# The Last ~~Laugh Joke Book~~

## A Collection of Inappropriate, Offensive and NSFW Jokes

### By Alex Newman

ISBN-13: 978-1539841647

ISBN-10: 1539841642

# Table of Contents

# Introduction and Content Warning

**Buy a book, laugh your ass off, help a guy out.**

My name is Alex. Over a year ago, my ex left me, after screwing me over personally and financially. I had no legal fight to challenge what happened. I was at an emotional and financial loss. She left me high and dry, left me in debt, and left me feeling I couldn't trust anyone or anything. I found out later I wasn't the first guy she did this to either.

I could have thrown in the towel. I could have wallowed in self-pity or grief. Instead, I chose to laugh.

I started reading jokes online. But not clean jokes. I read the dirty jokes, inappropriate jokes, jokes you could never tell at work. These are the jokes that are funny as hell (but without crossing the gone-too-far line).

I complied all of the wonderful jokes I found here. There are sex jokes, men/women jokes, gay jokes, religion jokes, and more. There are quick punchline jokes and longer story jokes. One thing is for sure- they are all offensive. These jokes are not appropriate for work or for children.

I decided to put together this joke book. If I can sell enough copies of this book to pay off the debt she left me, while making other people laugh, it will be the closure and happy ending I need to move on and recover from the damage done.

**This joke book contains offensive, dark, and sexual jokes and is not appropriate for anyone under the age of 21. If you are easily offended, this is not the book for you.**

Thank you for getting this book, for telling your friends about it, and for joining me in getting the last laugh.

-Alex

# One-Liners and Quick Jokes

I tried phone sex once, but the holes were too small.

How are tornadoes and marriage alike? They both begin with a lot of sucking and blowing, and in the end you lose your house.

Why did the snowman smile? Because the snow blower is coming.

Without nipples, breasts would be pointless.

What do you call a cheap circumcision? A rip off.

What's the definition of a Yankee? Same thing as a "quickie," only you do it to yourself.

Why doesn't Santa have any kids? He only comes once a year.

How is a push-up bra like a bag of chips? As soon as you open it, you realize it's half empty.

Why do female skydivers wear jock straps? So they don't whistle on the way down.

A man says to a woman, "Do you want to play lion tamer?" She asks: "What is that?" Man: "It's when you get on all fours and I

5

put my head in your mouth."

Mom to children: "I swear to drunk I'm not God, but seriously, stay in drugs, eat school, and don't do vegetables."

If someone notices you with an open zipper, answer proudly: "professional habit."

Missionary Impossible: When two fat people try to have sex.

Silence doesn't mean your sexual performance left her speechless.

I saw a woman wearing a sweat shirt with "Guess" on it. So I said, "Implants?"

Who can make more money in a week, a drug dealer or a prostitute? The prostitute because she can wash and resell her crack.

What is the difference between a dog and a fox? About five drinks.

When I was a kid my mother stopped breast feeding me. I asked her why and she said, "Hey, I just wanna be friends."

What is the difference between a vitamin and a hormone? You

can't make a vitamin.

What's the difference between a pregnant woman and a lightbulb? You can unscrew a lightbulb.

A man is driving down the road when a cop pulls him over. The cop says, "Hey pal your wife fell out of the car a few blocks back!" The man says, "Thank God. I thought I went deaf."

What's the best part about gardening? Getting down and dirty with your hoes.

What do you call a truckload of vibrators? Toys for Twats.

What do soybeans and dildos have in common? Both are meat substitutes.

What do you call an Amish guy with his arm up a horse's ass? A mechanic.

Why do vegetarians give good head? Because they're used to eating nuts.

A chicken and an egg are lying in bed. The chicken happily smokes while the egg looks a bit pissed off. The egg mutters, "Well, I guess we answered THAT question!"

Why do walruses love a Tupperware party? They're always on the lookout for a tight seal.

What's the difference between your boyfriend and a condom? Condoms have evolved: They're not so thick and insensitive anymore.

How is being in the military like getting a blowjob? The closer you get to discharge, the better you feel.

What did the egg say to the boiling water? "It will take a minute for me to get hard- I just got laid by a chick."

Did you hear about the blind prostitute? Well, you got to hand it to her.

What is a zebra? 26 sizes larger than an "A" bra.

Scooters are for men who want to ride motorcycles, but prefer to feel the wind on their vaginas.

I tried to be polite and hold the door open for a woman, but she kept screaming, "I'm peeing in here!"

I think the only time my ex didn't fake an orgasm was when the judge signed the divorce papers.

What is the difference between snowmen and snowwomen? Snowballs.

What has a whole bunch of little balls and screws old ladies? A bingo machine.

I feel like a Tampax – at a good place, but wrong time...

What's "68"? You do me and I owe you one.

FRIDAY is my second favorite "F" word.

What do you call a guy who cries when he masturbates? A tearjerker.

Success is like pregnancy. Everybody congratulates you, but nobody knows how many times you got fucked to achieve it.

Sex on television can't hurt unless you fall off.

Can you say three two-letter words that mean small? "Is it in?"

How are airplanes and women alike? They both have cockpits.

A man came up with a new invention- a vibrating tampon. That way a woman can be at her best when she is at her worst.

What do toys and boobs have in common? Both are made for children but it's the fathers who play with them the most.

Why do they say that eating yogurt and oysters will improve your sex life? Because if you'll eat that stuff, you'll eat anything.

Teenage daughter to mother: "Mom, does the rhythm method work?" Mom: "Go ask your brother."

Did you hear about the blind gynecologist? He reads lips.

During sex, my girlfriend always wants to talk to me. Just the other night she called me from a hotel.

If you're looking for sympathy, you'll find it in the dictionary between "shit" and "syphilis."

I run faster horny than you do scared.

Why did God give men penises? So they'd have at least one way to shut a woman up.

My birth certificate was a letter of apology that my dad got from the condom company.

What does tightrope walking and getting a blowjob from Grandma have in common? You don't look down.

What is it when a woman talks dirty to a man? $3.99 a minute.

If God hadn't meant the pussy to be eaten, he wouldn't have made it look like a taco.

Why does the bride always wear white? Because it is good for the dishwasher to match the stove and the refrigerator.

Sex at age 90 is like trying to shoot pool with a rope.

How did the Burger King get the Dairy Queen pregnant? He forgot to wrap his whopper.

What did the hurricane say to the palm tree? "Better hold onto your nuts because this is no ordinary blowjob."

What's the difference between a joke and two dicks? You can't take a joke.

Don't hate me because I'm beautiful. Hate me because your boyfriend thinks so.

What goes in hard and dry, but comes out soft and wet? Gum.

Impotence: Nature's way of saying, "No hard feelings."

What do you call a virgin on a water bed?  A cherry float.

My girlfriend's dad asked me what I do. Apparently, "your daughter" wasn't the right answer.

Why don't bunnies make noise when they have sex? Because they have cotton balls.

What do you call it when a 90-year-old man masturbates successfully? Miracle whip.

Let's both be naughty this year and save Santa the trip.

What's the difference between Tiger Woods and Santa? Santa stopped at three "ho's."

My girlfriend told me to go out and get something that makes her look sexy... so I got drunk.

I sent an angel to watch over you last night but he came back saying he can't watch porn.

You cannot play with me unless you blow me. –Balloon

My favorite sexual position: The Chilean miner. That's where you go down on me and stay there until Christmas.

Hear the slogan for the Stealth Condom? "They'll never see you coming."

What do a Rubik's Cube and a penis have in common? The more you play with it, the harder it gets.

If you love a woman, you shouldn't be ashamed to show her to your wife.

My mom asked me if I was bringing a date to Thanksgiving dinner. I said no, all my boyfriends like to spend Thanksgiving with their wives.

What's the difference between being hungry and being horny? Where you put the cucumber.

What did Cinderella do when she got to the ball? She gagged.

What's green and smells like pork?  Kermit the Frog's finger.

What is long, hard, and full of seamen? A submarine.

Why does Dr. Pepper come in a can? Because his wife died.

Why is a vagina just like the weather? When it's wet, it's time to go inside.

What do a dildo and tofu have in common? They are both meat substitutes.

Why isn't there a pregnant Barbie doll? Ken came in another box.

What's the difference between a tire and 365 used condoms? One's a Goodyear. The other's a great year.

Why does Miss Piggy douche with honey? Because Kermit likes sweet and sour pork.

What did the penis say to the vagina? "Don't make me come in there!"

My grandma told me her joints are getting weaker, so I told her to roll them tighter.

What's another name for a vagina? The box a penis comes in.

What's the difference between a pick-pocket and a peeping tom? One snatches your watch. The other watches your snatch.

What's the difference between your dick and a bonus check? Someone's always willing to blow your bonus.

What do you call a policewoman who shaves her pubes?
Cuntstubble.

Why do Driver's Ed classes in redneck schools use the car only on Mondays, Wednesdays, and Fridays? Because on Tuesday and Thursday, the Sex Ed class uses it.

What's the difference between a southern zoo and a northern zoo? The southern zoo has a description of the animal- along with a recipe.

What did the O say to the Q? "Dude, your dick's hanging out."

What do you get when you mix birth control and LSD? A trip without kids.

Dating is a lot like fishing. Sure there's plenty of fish in the sea. But until I catch one, I'm just stuck here holding my rod.

My girlfriend says she doesn't trust me. I guess that's just one more thing she has in common with my wife.

Words can't describe how beautiful my girlfriend is. But numbers can... 2/10.

Three nuns are sitting on a park bench when a man in a trench coat runs up and flashes them. One of them immediately has a stroke; the other two couldn't reach.

What's the difference between a hippie woman and a hockey team? A hockey team showers after three periods.

A guy walks into a bar with a .44 magnum and yells, "Who the hell fucked my wife!" Everybody's silent for a second. Then a guy in the back of the bar says, "You haven't got enough bullets, buddy."

A single guy walked up to a woman in a bar and said, "You are the most beautiful thing I have ever seen. I want you for my wife." She says, "Oh, okay. Where is she?"

What do you call kids born in whorehouses? Brothel sprouts.

Have you heard about the new mint-flavored birth control pill for women that they take immediately before sex? They're called "Predickamints."

Why didn't the toilet paper cross the road? It got stuck in a crack.

What is the difference between a genealogist and a gynecologist? A genealogist looks up your family tree, whereas a gynecologist looks up your family bush.

What's the process of applying for a job at Hooters? They just give you a bra and say, "Here, fill this out."

One day, a little boy wrote to Santa Claus, "Please send me a sister." Santa Claus wrote him back, "Okay, send me your mother."

How is pubic hair like parsley? You push it to the side before you start eating.

What did the blind man say when he passed the fish market? "Good morning ladies."

What do a gynecologist and a pizza delivery driver have in common? They can both smell it but they can't taste it.

My mother never saw the irony in calling me a son-of-a-bitch.

A sex toy store was robbed. Police are probing witnesses.

I had sex with a girl in an apple orchard once. I came in cider.

I'm emotionally constipated. I haven't given a shit in days.

Why is sleeping with a man like a soap opera? Just when it's getting interesting, they're finished until next time.

Ever had sex while camping? It's fucking intents.

What is the difference between "ooooooh" and "ooowwww?" About three inches.

What does a perverted frog say? Rubbit.

Why are pubic hairs so curly? So they don't poke her eye out.

What's the difference between medium and rare?  Six inches is medium, ten inches is rare.

What's the difference between a G-Spot and a golf ball? A guy will actually search for a golf ball.

# Blonde Jokes

Why does a blond wear a tight skirt? To keep her legs closed.

Why do blondes wear underwear? To keep their ankles warm.

A blonde and a brunette were talking one day. The brunette said that her boyfriend had a slight dandruff problem but she gave him "Head and Shoulders" and it cleared it up. The blonde asked inquisitively: "How do you give shoulders?"

What do blondes and railroad tracks have in common? They've both been laid all over America.

Two little boys, one blond and one with brown hair, were arguing over whose father could beat the other's father up. The brown-haired boy said, "My father is way better than yours." The blond replied, "Maybe, but my mother is better than yours." The brown-haired boy replied, "That's what my father says."

What do you say to a blonde that won't give in? "Have another beer."

Why do blondes wear green lipstick? Because red means stop.

What do you call a blonde with pigtails? A blowjob with handlebars.

How does the blond turn on the light after sex? She opens the car door.

What do you call two nuns and a blonde? Two tight ends and a wide receiver.

What does a screen door and a blonde have in common? The more you bang it, the looser it gets.

Why did the blonde take more than one pregnancy test? Because she slept with more than one guy.

A blonde walks into a drugstore and purchases a pack of condoms. "That will be $1.08, please," says the clerk. "What are the eight cents for?" asks the blonde. "It says one dollar right here on the packaging." "Tax," replies the clerk. "Gee," says the blonde, "I thought you just rolled them on and they stayed put by themselves."

Why did the blonde have a triangular coffin? Because as soon as her head hits a pillow she spreads her legs!

What do you give the blonde that has everything? Penicillin.

What does the Bermuda Triangle and blondes have in common? They've both swallowed a lot of seamen.

Three blondes are in the woods. The first blonde says, "These are deer tracks." The second blonde says, "No, these are bear tracks." The third blonde says, "No they are not. They are…" And they all get hit by the train.

A redhead tells her blonde stepsister, "I slept with a Brazilian...." The blonde replies, "Oh my God! You slut! How many is a brazilian?"

Did you hear about the blonde with a PhD in Psychology? She'll blow your mind, too.

What's the difference between a blonde woman and a gay guy? The blonde has the higher sperm count.

Did you hear about the new blonde paint? It's not real bright, but it's cheap, and spreads easy.

What do you call a blonde with a dollar on the top of her head? All you can eat, under a buck.

Did you hear about the conceited blonde? She screams her own name when she comes.

Why can't blondes count to 70? Because 69 is a bit of a mouthful.

A blonde walked into the dentist office and sat down in the chair. The dentist said, "Open wide!" "I can't," the blonde said. "This chair has arms."

A man and a blonde woman were waiting at the hospital donation center. The man asked her, "What are you doing here today?" The blonde woman replied, "Oh, I'm here to donate some blood. They're going to give me $5 for it." The man responded, "Hmm, that's interesting. I'm here to donate sperm, myself. But they pay me $25." The woman looked thoughtful for a moment, and they chatted some more before going their separate ways. A couple months later, the same man and woman meet again in the donation center. The man saw her and said, "Oh, hi there! Here to donate blood again?" The blonde woman shook her head with her mouth closed and mumbled, "Unh unh."

A blonde, brunette and a redhead are at the gynecologist. They are all pregnant. The brunette says, "I'm having a boy because I was on top." The red head says, "Well I'm having a girl because I was on the bottom." They both look over to the blonde and the blonde says, "I guess I'm having a puppy."

A blonde goes to an international message center to call her mother. When the man tells her it will be $300, she exclaims, "I don't have that kind of money, but I'll do ANYTHING to get a message to my mother." He tells the blonde to follow him and takes her into a back room. He unzips his pants and takes out his penis. The blonde gets on her knees, brings it toward her mouth and says, "Hello? Mom?"

What's a blonde's favorite nursery rhyme? "Humpme Dumpme."

A blonde picks up her dress from the dry cleaners. When she leaves, the cashier says, "Come again!" The blonde replies, "Nah. It was ketchup this time."

What does a blonde and a turtle have in common? If either one of them ends up on their back, they are both fucked.

What's the difference between a chorus line of blondes and a magician? A magician has a cunning array of stunts.

Why don't blondes like anal sex? They don't like their brains being screwed with.

What is the best blonde secretary in the world to have? One that never misses a period.

What's the difference between a bowling ball and a blonde? You can only fit three fingers inside a bowling ball.

A blonde and a brunette walk past a flower shop and see the brunette's boyfriend buying flowers. She sighs and says, "Oh crap, my boyfriend is buying me flowers again. Now, I'll be expected to spend the weekend on my back with my legs in the air." The blonde says, "Don't you have a vase?"

A brunette, a blonde and a redhead are all in fifth grade. Who has the biggest tits? The blonde, because she's 20.

A cop saw a car weaving all over the road and pulled it over. He walked up to the car and saw a blonde woman behind the wheel. There was a strong smell liquor on her breath. He said, "I'm going to give you a breathalyzer test to determine if you are under the influence of alcohol." She did the breathalyzer test and he walked it back to the police car. After a couple of minutes, he returned to her car and said, "It looks like you've had a couple of stiff ones." The blonde replied, "You mean it shows that, too?"

# Men/Women Jokes

Why are men are like public toilets? The good ones are taken, and the rest are full of shit.

The only reason the term "Ladies first" was invented was for the guy to check out the woman's ass.

When a man falls off a boat, you yell, "Man overboard!" What do you yell if a woman falls overboard? "Full speed ahead!"

How do you fix a woman's watch? Why should you? There's a clock on the oven.

Why did God create the orgasm? So women can moan even when they're happy.

Why do men find it difficult to make eye contact? Breasts don't have eyes.

Do you know why women fake orgasms? Because men fake foreplay.

If a woman is cold as a fish, a man has to be as patient as a fisherman.

Why do men become smarter during sex? Because they are plugged into a genius.

Why are men like cars? Because they always pull out before they check to see if anyone else is coming.

Why did God put men on the Earth? Because a vibrator can't mow the lawn.

What is the difference between men and women? A woman wants one man to satisfy her every need, and a man wants every woman to satisfy his one need.

Men will brag that there are women waiting by the phone at this very moment for their call. Who are these women? Women working at 900 numbers.

A boy asks his dad what the difference between a pussy and a cunt is? The dad points at his wife's crotch and says, "That's a pussy, the rest is a cunt."

What is the one thing that all men at singles bars have in common? They're married.

What is the difference between a battery and a woman? A battery has a positive side.

How is a girlfriend like a laxative?  They both irritate the shit out of you.

What do you call the useless piece of skin on a dick?  The man.

Why does a penis have a hole in the end?  So men can be open minded.

A man is talking to a woman in a bar.
He says, "What's your name?"
She says, "Carmen."
He says, "That's a nice name. Who named you, your mother?"
She says, "No, I named myself."
He says, "Why Carmen?"
She says, "Because I like cars and I like men. What's your name?"
He says, "Beertits."

Why are hurricanes normally named after women?  When they come they're wild and wet, but when they go they take your house and car with them.

Why do women rub their eyes when they get up in the morning? They don't have balls to scratch.

What do women and noodles have in common? Both wiggle when

you eat them.

As an airplane is about to crash, a female passenger jumps up frantically and announces, "If I'm going to die, I want to die feeling like a woman." She removes all her clothing and asks, "Is there someone on this plane who is man enough to make me feel like a woman?" A man stands up, removes his shirt and says, "Here, iron this!"

The newlyweds are in their honeymoon room, and the groom decides to let the bride know where she stands right from the start of the marriage. He proceeds to take off his pants and throw them at her. He says, "Put those on." The bride replies, "I can't wear your pants." He replies, "And don't forget that! I will always wear the pants in the family!" The bride takes off her panties and throws them at him with the same request, "Try those on!" He replies, "I can't get into your panties!" She replies, "And you never will if you don't realize I'm in charge."

A guy walks into a sperm donor bank wearing a ski mask and holding a gun, walking up with a woman. He goes up to the nurse and demands her to open the sperm bank vault. She says, "But sir, it's just a sperm bank!" He replies, "I don't care, open it now!" So she opens the door to the vault and inside are all the sperm samples. The guy says, "Take one of those sperm samples and drink it!" She looks at him and gasps, "BUT, they are sperm samples!" The man screams, "Do it!" So the nurse sucks it back. The man points to the next sample. "That one there, drink that one as well!" So the nurse drinks that one as well. The man takes off his ski mask, turns to the woman he walked in with, and says, "See honey, you can swallow too – it's not that hard!"

A man and his new bride enter their honeymoon sweet, and he is very nervous. They had decided to wait until after they were married to consummate the relationship. As he began to undress in front of his new wife, she notices that his toes are deformed, and she stares at his feet. He said to his bride, "I see know notice my feet. When I was young I had a disease called Toelio." His wife says, "You mean you had Polio?" He replies, "No, Toelio- it is a rare disease that effects your feet." As he takes off his pants, she notices that his knees are deformed as well. He sees her looking and tells her, "I also had Kneasles." His bride says to him, "Don't know mean Measles?" He replies, "No, Kneasles is a rare disease that impacts you knees." Nervously, he takes off the rest of his clothing. When his shorts come off, she looks at him and says: "Oh, I see you had Small Cox too!"

# Married Couple Jokes

An old man goes to the Wizard to ask him if he can remove a curse he has been living with for the last 40 years. The Wizard says, "Maybe, but you will have to tell me the exact words that were used to put the curse on you." The old man says without hesitation, "I now pronounce you man and wife."

A couple is lying in bed. The man says to his wife, "I am going to make you the happiest woman in the world." The woman says, "I'll miss you."

Never get on one knee for a girl who won't get on two for you.

Jack is on his death bed, and he says to his wife, "Can you give me one last wish?" She says, "Anything you want." He says, "After I die, will you marry Larry?" She says, "But I thought you hated Larry." With his last breath, he says, "I do."

A man is out shopping and he finds a new brand of Olympic condoms. Impressed, he buys a pack. When he gets home he tells his wife about the purchase he just made. "Olympic condoms?" she blurts, "What makes them so special?" "There are three colors," he replies, "Gold, Silver and Bronze." "What color are you going to wear tonight?" she asks cheekily. "Gold of course," says the man proudly. The wife responds, "Why don't you wear Silver. It would be nice if you came second for a change!"

A couple drove down a country road, not saying a word to each other after a nasty fight. As they passed a barnyard of mules and pigs, the wife sarcastically asked, "Relatives of yours?" "Yep," the husband replied. "In-laws."

A man had just finished reading a new book entitled, "You Can Be the Man of Your House." He stormed to his wife in the kitchen and announced, "From now on, you need to know that I am the man of this house and my word is law. You will prepare me a gourmet meal tonight, and when I'm finished eating my meal, you will serve me a sumptuous dessert. After dinner, you are going to go upstairs with me and we will have the kind of sex that I want. Afterwards, you are going to draw me a bath so I can relax. You will wash my back and towel me dry and bring me my robe. Then, you will massage my feet and hands. Then tomorrow, guess who's going to dress me and comb my hair?" His wife replied, "The fucking funeral director would be my first guess."

A husband comes home to find his wife with her suitcases packed in the living room. "Where the hell do you think you're going?" he says. She replies, "I'm going to Las Vegas. You can earn $500 for a blow job there, and I figured that I might as well earn money for what I do to you free." The husband thinks for a moment, goes upstairs, and comes back down, with his suitcase packed as well. "Where do you think you going?" the wife asks. "I'm coming with you," he replies. "I want to see how you survive on $1,000 a year!"

A pregnant woman visited her obstetrician's office. After the exam, she shyly said, "My husband wants me to ask you..." The doctor stops her and says, "I know...I know..." and places a reassuring hand on her shoulder. "I get asked that all the time. Sex is fine until late in the pregnancy." "No, that's not it," the woman responds. "He wants to know if I can still mow the lawn."

A young couple, on the brink of divorce, visits a marriage counselor. The counselor asks the wife: "What's the problem?" She responds: "My husband suffers from premature ejaculation." The counselor turns to her husband and inquires: "Is that true?" The husband replies: "Well, not exactly. She's the one that suffers, not me."

Two married buddies are out drinking one night when one turns to the other and says, "You know, I don't know what else to do. Whenever I go home after we've been out drinking, I turn the headlights off before I get to the driveway. I shut off the engine and coast into the garage. I take my shoes off before I go into the house, I sneak up the stairs, I get undressed in the bathroom. I ease into bed and my wife STILL wakes up and yells at me for staying out so late!" His buddy looks at him and says, "Well, you're obviously taking the wrong approach. I screech into the driveway, slam the door, storm up the steps, throw my shoes into the closet, jump into bed, rub my hands on my wife's ass and say, 'How about a blowjob?' And she's always sound asleep."

As a couple gets into bed, the husband starts to rub and kiss his wife. She turns over and says, "I'm sorry, honey. I've got a gynecologist appointment tomorrow, and I want to stay fresh." The husband sadly turns over. A few minutes later, he rolls back over and taps his wife. "Do you have a dentist appointment, too?"

An old man and his wife were watching a healing service on the television. The evangelist called out to all who wanted to be healed to go to their television set, place one hand on the TV and the other hand on the body part where they wanted to be healed. The old woman got up and slowly hobbled to the television set, placed her right hand on the set, and her left hand on her arthritic shoulder, which was causing her great pain. Then the old man got up, went to the TV, and placed his right hand on the set and his

33

left hand on his crotch. The old woman scowled at him and said, "I guess you just don't get it. The purpose of doing this is to heal the sick, not raise the dead."

What's the difference between a girlfriend and a wife? 45 pounds.

A man walks into his bedroom with a sheep under his arm. His wife is lying in bed reading. The man says, "This is the pig I have sex with when you've got a headache." The wife replies, "That is a sheep." The man replies, "I was talking to the sheep."

What do you call a woman who is paralyzed from the waist down? Married.

Why did the woman leave her husband after he got a penis enlarger? She just couldn't take it any longer.

One morning, a doctor and his wife were having a big argument about their sex life. "You aren't so good in bed either!" he shouted and stormed off to work. By mid-morning, he decided he'd better make amends and called home. The wife picked the phone after several rings. "What took you so long to answer?" the husband asked. She replied, "I was in bed." "What were you doing in bed this late?" She answered, "Getting a second opinion."

A man and his wife go to their honeymoon hotel for their 25th anniversary. As the couple thought about their wedding night and the first time they had sex, the wife asked the husband, "When you first saw my naked body in front of you, what was going through your mind?" The husband replied, "All I wanted to do was to fuck your brains out, and suck your tits dry." Then, she asked, "What are you thinking now?" He replied, "It looks as if I did a pretty good job."

How can you tell if your wife is dead? The sex is the same but the dishes pile up.

A husband emerged from the bathroom naked and was climbing into bed when his wife complained, as usual, "I have a headache." "Perfect," her husband said. "I was just in the bathroom powdering my penis with aspirin. You can take it orally or as a suppository, it's up to you!"

A young boy and his father were in a store when they walked past a rack of condoms. Curious, the boy asked his father, "What are these things daddy?" His dad said, "Condoms, son." The boy asked, "Why do they come in packs of 1,3, and 12?" The dad replied, "The packs with one are for the high school boys, one for Saturday night. The ones with three are for the college boys, one

35

for Friday, Saturday and Sunday night. And the ones with twelve in them are for the married men, one for each month of the year."

As a painless way to save money, a young couple arranged that every time they have sex, the husband puts his pocket change into a piggy bank on the bedside table. One night while being unusually athletic, he accidentally knocked the piggy bank onto the floor, and it shattered into several pieces. To his surprise, among the masses of coins, there are handfuls of five and ten dollar bills. He asks his wife, "What's up with all the bills?" His wife replies, "Well, not everyone is as cheap as you are."

A guy comes home from work, walks into his bedroom, and finds a stranger fucking his wife. He says, "What the hell are you two doing?" His wife turns to the stranger and says, "I told you he was stupid."

A man and a woman were celebrating their 50th anniversary. They were talking before their dinner about how they should celebrate their big evening. The woman decided she would cook a big dinner for her husband. Then he said they should do what they did on their wedding night- eat at the dinner table naked. The woman agreed. Later that night at the table, the woman said, "Honey, my nipples are as hot for you as they were fifty years ago." The man replied, "That's because they are sitting in your soup."

A boy was walking down the street when he noticed his grandpa sitting on the porch, in the rocking chair, with nothing on from the waist down. "Grandpa what are you doing?" he exclaimed. The old man looked off in the distance and did not answer him. "Grandpa, what are you doing sitting out here with nothing on below the waist?" he asked again. The old man slowly looked at him and said, "Well, last week I sat out here with no shirt on, and I got a stiff neck. This is your Grandma's idea."

A husband and wife went to take golf lessons from a pro at a local country club. The man and woman meet the pro and head onto the driving range. The man goes up to hit first. He swings and hits the ball 100 yards. The golf pro says, "Not bad. Now hold the club as firm as you hold your wife's breasts." The man follows instructions and hits the ball 300 yards. The golf pro says "Excellent!" Now the woman takes her turn. Her ball goes 30 yards. The golf pro says, "Not bad. Try holding the club like you hold your husband's dick." She swings and the ball goes 10 yards. The golf pro says, "Not bad, but now try taking the club out of your mouth."

A husband and his wife who have been married 20 years were outside doing some yard work. The man was working hard cleaning the BBQ grill while his wife was bending over, weeding flowers from the flower bed. The man says to his wife, "Your rear end is almost as wide as this grill!" She ignores the remark. A little later, the husband takes his measuring tape and measures the grill, then he goes over to his wife while she is bending over, measures her rear end and gasps, "Geez, it really IS as wide as the grill!" She ignores this remark as well. Later that night while in bed, her husband starts to feel frisky. The wife calmly responds, "If you think I'm gonna fire up the grill for one little wiener, you are sadly mistaken."

A man phones home from his office and says to his wife, "I have the chance to go fishing for a week. It's the opportunity of a lifetime. I have to leave right away. Pack my clothes, my fishing equipment, and especially my blue silk pajamas. I'll be home in an hour to pick them up." The man rushes home to grab everything. He hugs his wife, apologizes for the short notice, and then hurries off. A week later, the man returns and his wife asks, "Did you have a good trip, dear?" The man replies, "Yep, the fishing was great... but you forgot to pack my blue silk pajamas." His wife smiles and says, "Oh, no I didn't... I put them in your tackle box!"

An old man was laying on his death bed. With only hours to live, he suddenly noticed the scent of chocolate chip cookies coming from the kitchen. With his last bit of energy, the old man pulled himself out from his bed, across the floor to the stairs, and down the stairs to the kitchen. There, the old man's wife was baking chocolate chip cookies. With his last ounce of energy, the old man reached for a cookie. His wife, however, quickly smacked him across the back of his hand, and shouted, "Leave them alone, they're for the funeral!"

A woman came up behind her husband while he was enjoying his morning coffee and slapped him on the back of the head. "I found a piece of paper in your pants pocket with the name 'Marylou' written on it," she said, furious. "You had better have an explanation." "Calm down, honey," the man replied. "Remember last week when I was at the horse track? That was the name of the horse I bet on." The next morning, his wife snuck up on him and smacked him again, "What was that for?" he complained. She replied, "Your horse called on the phone last night."

An elderly woman got sick and tired of her husband farting uncontrollably every morning when he woke up. She told him, "You're going to fart your guts out one of these days." He ignored her warning and continued farting each morning. She finally decided that she was going to teach her husband a lesson, and placed turkey guts by his backside while he was asleep. She left the bedroom and went downstairs to make breakfast when she heard his usual loud farting, only this time it was followed by a blood-curdling scream. A few minutes later, the old man came downstairs visibly shaking and said, "You were right! I DID fart out my guts, but by the grace of God and these two fingers, I pushed them back in."

Two men are talking together at a restaurant. They're discussing the state of marriage today. One man says, "I didn't sleep with my wife before we were married. Did you?" The other man replies, "I'm not sure. What was your wife's maiden name?"

A man walked into a bar and asks the bartender for ten shots of whiskey. The bartender asks, "What's the matter?" The man says, "I found out my brother is gay and marrying my best friend." The next day, the same man comes in and orders 12 shots of whiskey. The bartender asks, "What's wrong this time?" The man says, "I found out that my son is gay." The next day, the same man comes in the bar and orders 15 shots of whiskey. Then the bartender asks, "Doesn't anyone in your family like women?" The man looks up and says, "Apparently my wife does."

A guy goes into a tattoo parlor and asks for a tattoo of a $100 bill on his penis. Curious, the tattoo artist asks him why he would possibly want that. The man responds- "Three reasons: I like to play with my money, I like to watch my money grow, and a hundred dollars seems to be the only thing my wife will blow these days."

A newly married sailor was informed by the Navy that he was going to be stationed a long way from home on a remote island in the Pacific for a year. A few weeks after he got there he began to miss his new wife, so he wrote her a letter. "My love," he wrote, "We are going to be apart for a very long time. Already I'm starting to miss you and there's really not much to do here in the evenings. Besides that, we're constantly surrounded by young attractive native girls. Do you think if I had a hobby of some kind I would not be tempted?" So his wife sent him back a harmonica saying, "Why don't you learn to play this?" Eventually his tour of duty came to an end and he rushed back to his wife. "Darling" he said, "I can't wait to get you into bed so that we make passionate love!" She kissed him and said, "First let's see you play that harmonica."

A guy stands over his golf tee shot for what seems an eternity:

looking up, looking down, measuring the distance, figuring the wind direction and speed. Finally, his exasperated partner says, "What's taking so long? Hit the damn ball!" The guy answers, "My wife is up there watching me from the clubhouse. I want to make this a perfect shot." "Forget it, man," says his golf partner. "You'll never hit her from here."

A man was complaining to a friend, "I had it all! Money, a magnificent house, a fast car, the love of a beautiful woman... then, poof! It was all gone!" "What happened?" asked the friend. The man replied, "My wife found out."

A man and his wife were celebrating their 50th wedding anniversary. The wife says to her husband, "For our anniversary this year, you can ask me one question, any question you want to. I will answer it truthfully." The husband replies, "Okay, this has been bothering me for a long time, but I haven't had the courage to ask before. I have noticed that all of our eight children look similar to each other except one. I can't figure out how he got to look so different. Did he have a different father than the rest?" The wife stops. She is unable to look her husband in the eyes. Slowly she replies, "Yes. He did have a different father." Her husband was taken aback. "Oh! Okay... I must know. Please tell me. Who was that child's father?" Again she cannot look her husband in the eyes. She is very distressed, and after a long silence she slowly said, "YOU."

A man was talking to his friend. He said, "I don't know what to get my wife for her birthday - she has everything, and besides, she can afford to buy anything she wants, so I'm stumped." His friend said, "I have an idea - why don't you make up a certificate saying she can have 60 minutes of great sex, any way she wants it. She'll probably be thrilled." So the man did. The next day his friend said, "Well? Did you take my suggestion?" "Yes, I did," said the man. "Did she like it?" His friend asked. "Oh yes! she jumped up, thanked me, kissed me on the forehead and ran out the door, yelling 'I'll be back in an hour!"

A couple was celebrating their 25th wedding anniversary at home with a couple of bottles of champagne. A bit tipsy and feeling very intimate the husband turns to his wife and asks, "Tell me truthfully, have you ever been unfaithful to me?" "Well," she replied, "since you ask, to tell you the truth I have been unfaithful on three occasions." The man is shocked. "What? How could you?" "Let me tell you about it," she said. "The first time was back when we were first married. You needed open heart surgery and we didn't have the money, so I went to bed with the surgeon and got him to operate for free." The man pauses to think and replies, "Gee! That was noble of you. And, besides, I guess I should be grateful. But, tell me, what about the second time?" She tells him, "Do you remember that you wanted that promotion at work, and they were going to pass you over for someone else? Well, I went to bed with the president and the vice president and they gave you the job." The man is upset for a second, but then he thinks about it and says, "Hell, I think I could have done it on my own. But, then again, I guess I should be grateful. And so, what about the third time?" The wife responds, "Do you remember two years ago when you wanted to become president of the baseball team, and you were missing 53 votes?"

A couple was married for 20 years. Every time they had sex, the husband always insisted on shutting off the lights. Well, after 20 years, the wife felt this was stupid. She figured she would break him of the crazy habit. So one night, while they were in the middle of doing it, she suddenly turned on the lights. She looked down and saw her husband was holding a dildo. She gets completely upset, and screams, "You impotent bastard!" She yelled at him, "How could you be lying to me all of these years. You better explain yourself!" The husband looks her straight in the eyes and says, calmly, "I'll explain the dildo if you can explain our three kids."

On their first night together, a newlywed couple go to change. The new bride comes out of the bathroom showered and wearing a beautiful robe. The proud husband says, "My dear, we are married now, you can open your robe." The beautiful young woman opens her robe, and he is astonished. "Oh," he exclaims, "My God you are so beautiful, let me take your picture." Puzzled, she asks, "My picture?" He answers, "Yes my dear, so I can carry your beauty next to my heart forever." She smiles and he takes her picture, and then he heads into the bathroom to shower. He comes out wearing his robe and the new wife asks, "Why do you wear a robe? We are married now." At that the man opens his robe and she exclaims, "Oh... oh my, let me get a picture." He beams and asks why and she answers, "So I can get it enlarged!"

A retired gentlemen went into the Social Security office to apply for Social Security. After waiting in line a long time he got to the counter. The woman behind the counter asked him for his driver's license to verify his age. He looked in his pockets and realized he had left his wallet at home. He told the woman that he was very sorry but he seemed to have left his wallet at home. "Will I have to go home and come back now?" he asks. The woman says, "Unbutton your shirt." He opens his shirt revealing lots of curly silver hair. She says, "That silver hair on your chest is proof enough for me," and she processed his Social Security application. When he gets home, the man excitedly tells his wife about his experience at the Social Security office. She said, "You should have dropped your pants- you might have qualified for disability, too."

A man and a woman had been married some time when the woman began to question her husband. She said, "I know you've been with a lot of woman before. How many were there?" The husband replied, "Look, I don't want to upset you, there were many. Let's just leave it alone." The wife continued to beg and plead. Finally, the husband gave in. "Let's see," he said. "There was one, two, three, four, five, six, you, eight, nine, ten..."

Every night after dinner, Harry took off for the local bar. He would spend the whole evening there and always arrive home, drunk, around midnight each night. He usually had trouble getting his key to fit the keyhole and couldn't get the door open. And, every time this happened, his wife would go to the door and let him in. Then, she would proceed to yell and scream at him for his constant nights out and coming home in a drunken state. But, Harry still continued his nightly routine.   One day, the distraught wife was talking to a friend about her husband's behavior. The friend listened and suggested, "Why don't you treat him a little differently when he comes home? Instead of berating him, why don't you give him some loving words and welcome him home with a kiss? Then, he might change his ways." The wife thought that this might be a good idea. That night, Harry took off again after dinner. And, at about midnight, he arrived home in his usual condition. His wife heard him at the door. She quickly opened it and let Harry in. Instead of berating him as she had always done, this time she took his arm and led him into the living room. She sat Harry down in an easy chair, put his feet up on the foot stool, and took his shoes off. Then, she went behind him and started to cuddle him a little. After a short while, she whispered to Harry, "It's pretty late, dear. I think we should go upstairs to bed now, don't you think?" Harry replied in his inebriated state, "Heck, I guess we might as well. I'll get in trouble when I get home anyway!"

A man is at work one day when he notices that his co-worker is wearing an earring. This man knows his co-worker to be a somewhat conservative fellow, so naturally he's curious about the sudden change in fashion sense. The man walks up to his co-worker and says, "I didn't know you were into earrings. How long have you been wearing an earring?" The man sheepishly replied, "Ever since my wife found it in my car."

A young girl gets married, and a few days later her mother comes to visit. When the mother arrives, she is shocked to find her daughter standing naked at the front door. "What are you doing!" shouts the mother. "Mom, it's my love dress! Don't you like it?" "I'll come back in a few weeks when the honeymoon is over," replies her mother, as she turns and leaves for the car. A few weeks later, the mother arrives at her daughter's house once. Again, she is shocked when her naked daughter answers the door to greet her. "Now what are you doing?" "Mom, it's my love dress! It keeps the marriage spicy!" "I'll give you a few more weeks," replies her mother, as she turns and leaves for the car. Later that night, the mother decides to try it for herself. When her husband arrives home, she greets him at the front door completely naked. "Honey, what are hell are you doing!" remarks the husband. "It's my love dress, dear! What do you think of it?" "Well, to be perfectly honest," replies her husband, "I think you should have ironed it first!"

A man left work one Friday afternoon. But, being payday, instead of going home, he stayed out the entire weekend partying with his friends, spending his entire paycheck. When he finally appeared at home on Sunday, he was confronted by his very angry wife and was barraged for nearly two hours. Finally, his wife stopped the nagging and simply said to him, "How would you like

48

it if you didn't see me for two or three days?" He replied. "That would be fine with me!" Monday went by and he didn't see his wife. Tuesday and Wednesday came and went with the same results. On Thursday, the swelling went down just enough where he could see her a little out of the corner of his left eye.

A man takes his wife to the stockyard animal show. They start heading down the alley that had the bulls. They come up to the first bull and his sign stated: "This bull mated 50 times last year." The wife turns to her husband and says, "He mated 50 times in a year, you could learn from him." They proceed to the next bull and his sign stated: "This bull mated 65 times last year." The wife turns to her husband and says, "This one mated 65 times last year. That is over five times a month. You can learn from this one, also." They proceeded to the last bull and his sign said: "This bull mated 365 times last year." The wife's mouth drops open and says, "Wow! He mated 365 times last year. That is once a day! You could really learn from this one." The man turns to his wife and says, "Go up and inquire if it was 365 times with the same cow."

A husband and wife are shopping in their local Wal-Mart. The husband picks up a case of Budweiser and puts it in their cart. "What do you think you're doing?" asks the wife. "They're on sale, only $10 for 24 cans," he replies. "Put them back, we can't afford them," demands the wife, and he does, then they carry on shopping. A few aisles later, the woman picks up a $20 jar of face cream and puts it in the basket. "What do you think you're doing?" asks the husband. "It's my face cream. It makes me look sexy and beautiful for you when we're making love," replies the wife. Her husband replies: "So does 24 cans of Budweiser- at half the price."

A police officer pulls a man over for speeding. As the officer approaches the car, he can see that the man is very anxious about something. The man opens his car window and the officer leans down. "Good afternoon sir," the officer says. "Do you know why I stopped you?" "Yes, officer... I know I was speeding -- but it is a matter of life or death." The cop is astonished. He says, "Oh, really? How's that?" The man replies, "There's a naked woman waiting for me at home." "I don't see how that is a matter of life or death." The man says- "If I don't get home before my wife does, I'm a dead man."

One night after watching "Who Wants to Be a Millionaire," a man and his wife went to bed. The man was getting very frisky. He asked his wife if she was in the mood. His wife answered, "Not tonight dear, I have a headache." The man replied, "Is that your final answer?" She said, "Yes." He said, "Okay, then I'd like to phone a friend."

A 54-year-old accountant left a letter for his wife one Friday evening that read: "Dear Wife, I am 54 and by the time you receive this letter I will be at the Grand Hotel with my beautiful and sexy 18-year-old secretary." When he arrived at the hotel, there was a letter waiting for him that read as follows: "Dear Husband, I too am 54 and by the time you receive this letter I will be at the Breakwater Hotel with my handsome and virile 18-year-old boy toy. And, you, being an accountant, will appreciate that 18 goes into 54 many more times than 54 goes into 18."

There are four kinds of sex.  There's House Sex: When you are newly married and have sex all over the house in every room. There's Bedroom Sex: After you have been married for a while, you only have sex in the bedroom.  There's Hall Sex: After you've been married for many, many years, you just pass each other in the hall and say "Fuck you!"  And then there's Courtroom Sex: When your wife and her lawyer fuck you in the divorce court in front of many people for every penny you've got.

George and Nancy decided to celebrate their 25th wedding anniversary with a trip to Las Vegas. When they entered the hotel

51

casino and registered, a sweet young woman dressed in a very short skirt became very friendly. George brushed her off. Nancy objected, "George, that young woman was nice, and you were so rude." He replied, "Dear, she's a prostitute." Nancy said, "I don't believe you. That sweet young thing?" George said, "Let's go up to our room and I'll prove it." In their room, George called down to the desk and asked for "Bambi" to come to room 1217. "Now," he said, "you hide in the bathroom with the door open just enough to hear us, okay?" Soon, there was a knock on the door. George opened it and a blonde walked in, swirling her hips provocatively. George asked, "How much do you charge?" The blonde replied, "$125 basic rate, $100 tips for special services." Even George was taken aback. "$125! I was thinking more in the range of $25." The woman laughed derisively. "You must really be a hick if you think you can buy sex for that price." "Well," said George, "I guess we can't do business. Good bye." After she left, Nancy came out of the bathroom. She said, "I just can't believe it!" George said, "Let's forget it. We'll go have a drink, then eat dinner." At the bar, as they sipped on their cocktails, the same woman came up behind George, pointed slyly at Nancy, and said, "See what you get for $25?"

# Sex Jokes

What's long and hard and has cum in it? A cucumber.

I'm trying to finish writing a script for a porno movie, but there are just too many holes in the plot.

What's the difference between oral sex and anal sex? Oral sex makes your day; anal sex makes your hole weak.

I was once in a jerking off contest. I took first... and third.

A lady walks into a sex shop, and yells out, "Where are all your dildos?" The salesperson answers, "They're on the wall behind me." The woman scans the wall, and then points and screams, "I'll take the red one!" The salesperson responds, "No lady... I there on the wall NEXT to the fire extinguisher."

Karma is like 69. You get what you give.

A woman walks into a drugstore and asks the pharmacist if he sells size extra-large condoms. He replies, "Yes we do. Would you like to buy some?" She responds, "No sir, but do you mind if I wait around here until someone does?"

A woman married and had 13 children. Her husband died. She married again and had seven more children. Again, her husband died. But, she remarried and this time had five more children. Alas, she finally died.  Standing before her coffin, the preacher prayed for her. He thanked the Lord for this very loving woman and said, "Lord, they're finally together."  One mourner leaned over and quietly asked her friend, "Do you think he means her first, second or third husband?" The friend replied, "I think he means her legs."

What did the banana say to the vibrator? "What are you shaking for? She's going to eat me!"

A man is in a hotel lobby. He wants to ask the clerk a question. As he turns to go to the front desk, he accidentally bumps into a woman beside him and as he does, his elbow goes into her breast. They are both startled and he says, "Ma'am, if your heart is as soft as your breast, I know you'll forgive me." She replies, "If your penis is as hard as your elbow, I'm in room 1221."

A woman walks into Wal-mart with her two children. The greeter welcomes her to Wal-mart, and casually asks if her children are twins. She says, "Twins? No, she is five and her brother is turning ten, why on earth would you think they were twins?" The greeter walked away shaking his head and mumbling, "I can't believe somebody screwed her twice."

As a woman passed her daughter's closed bedroom door, she heard a strange buzzing noise coming from within. Opening the door, she saw her daughter with a vibrator. Shocked, she asked: "What in the world are you doing?"  The daughter replied: "Mom, I'm forty years old, unmarried, and this thing is about as close as I'll ever get to a husband. Please, go away and leave me alone." The next day, the woman's father heard the same buzz coming from the other side of the closed bedroom door. Upon entering the room, he observed his daughter making passionate love to her vibrator. He asked what she was doing, and the daughter said: "Dad, I'm forty years old, unmarried, and this thing is about as close as I'll ever get to a husband. Please, go away and leave me alone."  A couple days later, the wife came home from a shopping trip.  She placed the groceries on the kitchen counter, and heard that buzzing noise coming from, of all places, the living room. She entered the room and saw her husband sitting on the couch, downing a cold beer, and staring at the TV. The vibrator was next to him on the couch, buzzing like crazy. The wife asked: "What the hell are you doing?"  The husband replied: "I'm watching football with my son-in-law."

A guy goes to a house of prostitution. He selects a girl, pays her $200 up front, and he gets undressed. She's about to take off her blue negligee, when the fire alarms sound throughout the house. She runs out of the room, with his $200 still in her hand. He quickly grabs his clothes and runs out after her. He's searching the building, but the smoke gets too heavy, so he runs outside looking for her. By this time, the firemen are there. He sees one of them and asks, "Did you see a beautiful blonde, in a sheer blue negligee, with $200 in her hand?" The fireman says, "No!" The guy then says, "Well if you see her, screw her. It's paid for."

A little boy walks up to his mother and asks a question. He had seen his parents having sex the night before, but didn't understand what they were doing. "Mommy, what were you doing bouncing on Daddy's stomach last night?" The mother replied, "I have to do that, or Daddy's belly gets very fat. Bouncing keeps him skinny." The little boy replies, "That's not going to work." The mother asks, "Why not?" The little boy says: "Because the babysitter keeps blowing him back up again."

A businessman was getting ready to go on a long business trip. He knew his wife was a flirtatious sort, so he thought he'd try to get her something to keep her occupied while he was away so she wouldn't be tempted to sleep with someone else. He went to a store that sold sex toys and started looking around. He thought about a life-sized sex doll, but that was too close to another man for him. He was browsing through the dildos, looking for something special to please his wife, and started talking to the old man behind the counter. He explained his situation, and the old man said, "Well, I don't really know of anything that will do the trick. We have vibrating dildos, special attachments, and so on, but I don't know of anything that will keep her occupied for weeks, except..." and he stopped.  The man said, "Except what?" The old man replied, "Nothing, nothing."  The man said, "Tell me! I need something!"  The old man replied, "Well, sir, I don't usually mention this, but there is the 'voodoo dick.'"  The old man reached under the counter, and pulled out an old wooden box, carved with strange symbols. He opened it, and there lay a very ordinary-looking dildo. The businessman laughed, and said, "Big fucking deal. It looks like every other dildo in this shop!"  "Ahh," the old man replied, "but you haven't seen what it'll do yet."  He pointed to a door and said, "Voodoo dick, the door."  The voodoo dick rose out of its box, darted over to the door, and started screwing the keyhole. The whole door shook with the vibrations, and a crack developed down the middle. Before the door split open, the old man said, "Voodoo dick, get back in your box!"  The voodoo dick stopped and floated back into the box.  The businessman screamed, "I'll take it!"  The old man resisted, saying it wasn't for sale, but he finally surrendered to $1,000 in cash. The businessman took it home to his wife, told her it was a special dildo and that to use it, all she had to do was say was, "Voodoo dick, my pussy." He left for his trip satisfied that things would be fine while he was gone.  After he'd been gone a few days, the wife was unbearably horny. She thought of several people who would willingly satisfy her, but then she remembered the voodoo dildo. She got it out, and said "Voodoo dick, my pussy!" The voodoo dildo shot to her crotch and started pumping. It was amazing- like nothing she'd ever experienced before.  After three orgasms, she decided she'd had enough, and tried to pull it out, but it was stuck in her, still thrusting. She tried and tried to get it out, but nothing worked. Her husband had forgot to tell her how to shut it off. So she decided to go to the hospital to see if they could help. She put her clothes on, got in the car and started to drive to the hospital, quivering with every thrust of the dildo.  On the way, another orgasm nearly made her swerve off the road, and she was pulled over by a policeman. He asked for her license, and then asked how much she'd had to drink. Gasping and twitching, she explained that she hadn't been drinking, but that a voodoo dick was stuck in her pussy, and wouldn't stop screwing her.  The officer looked at her for a second, and then said: "Yea, right. Voodoo dick, my ass!"

An Italian guy is out picking up chicks in Rome. While at his favorite bar, he manages to attract one rather attractive looking woman. They go back to his place, and they go at it. After a while, he climaxes loudly. Then he rolls over, lights up a cigarette and asks her, "So.... you finish?" After a slight pause. She replies, "No." Surprised, but pleasantly, he puts out his cigarette, rolls back on top of her, and has his way with her again, this time lasting even longer than the first. Again he rolls over, lights a cigarette, and asks, "So.... you finish?" And again, after a short pause, she simply says "No." Stunned, but still acting reflexively on his macho pride, he once again puts out the cigarette, and mounts her again. This time, with all the strength he could muster up, he barely manages to end the task, but he does, after quite some time and energy is spent. Barely able to roll over, he reaches for his cigarette, lights it again, and then asks tiredly, "So... you finish?" She replies, "No. I'm Swedish."

A father and his six-year-old son are walking down the street, and they come across two dogs having sex. The boy is shocked by what he sees and asks his father, "Daddy, what are they doing?"

The father, not wanting to lie to his son, says, "They're just making a puppy." "Okay," says the son, and the father is relieved that he doesn't probe further. The next day, the son bursts into his parents' room and sees them having sex. The father jumps up and quickly covers himself. Knowing he's in for an interesting talk, the father walks downstairs with his son and they sit at the dining room table. His son asks him, "Daddy, what were you and mommy doing?" Again, wanting to be honest with his son, he says, "Mommy and I were making a baby." His son pauses for a moment, thinking, and then replies, "Flip mommy over, I want a puppy!"

A man and a woman started to have sex in the middle of a dark forest. After about fifteen minutes of it, the man finally gets up and says, "Damn, I wish I had a flashlight!" The woman says, "Me too!  You've been eating grass for the past ten minutes!"

The Dean of Women at an exclusive girls' school was lecturing her students on sexual morality. "We live today in very difficult times for young people. In moments of temptation," she said. "Ask yourself just one question: Is an hour of pleasure worth a lifetime of shame?" A young woman rose her hand in the back of the room and said, "Excuse me, but how do you make it last an hour?"

A young bride-to-be asked her gynecologist to recommend some sort of contraceptive that would be an alternative to taking birth control pills. He suggested she try having her husband withdraw before he reaches orgasms, or using douches or condoms. Several years later, the woman was walking down the street with three children when she happened to run across her old doctor. "I see you decided not to take my advice," he said, eyeing the young children. "On the contrary, doctor," she exclaimed, "Dave here was a pullout, Danny was a washout, and Denise was a blowout!"

A man visits his doctor and says, "Doc, I think I've got a sex problem. I can't get... uh... aroused for my wife anymore." The doctor says, "Come back tomorrow and bring her with you." The next day, the guy shows up with his wife. The doctor says to the wife, "Take off your clothes and lie on the table." She does it, and the doctor walks around the table a few times looking her up and down. He looks at the man and says, "You're fine. She doesn't give me a hard-on, either."

A young man went into a drugstore to buy his first pack of condoms. There was a beautiful woman working behind the counter. The woman could tell the young man was not experienced with buying condoms as he walked back and forth in the aisle, staring nervously at all the packages. The woman

61

walked over to him and asked if he knew how to wear a condom. "No," the young man answered, "this is my first time." The woman took a condom package and opened it. She unwrapped the condom, took it out and slipped it over her thumb. She cautioned him to make sure it was on tight and secure. The young man still looked confused and nervous. So, she looked all around the store to make sure it was empty. "Just a minute," she said. She walked to the door, locked it, and put up a "Back in 15 Minutes" sign. Taking his hand, she led the young man into the back room. She unbuttoned her blouse and removed it. She unhooked her bra and laid it aside. "Do these excite you?" She asked. The young man nodded his head repeatedly. She then said it was time to slip the condom on. She dropped her skirt, removed her panties and lay down on a desk. "Well, come on," she said, "We don't have much time." The young man climbed on top of her. He got right to it, and was done within a few moments. She looked at him with a frown and said, "Did you put that condom on?" He replied, "I sure did!" Then he held up his thumb to show her. She fainted.

Jenny got the news that her elderly grandfather had died, and she went straight to visit her grandmother. When she asked how her grandpa had died, her grandma explained, not holding back anything of course, "He had a heart attack during sex, Sunday morning!" Horrified, Jenny suggested that having sex after 90 years old was surely asking for trouble. "Oh no," her grandma replied. "We had sex every Sunday morning in time with the church bells! In with the dings, out with the dongs!" She paused to wipe away a tear, and said, "And then, an ice cream truck drove by..."

An elderly man goes to his doctor and says, "Doctor, I need to I have my sex drive lowered!" The doctor replies, "But you are 91 years old. It's all in your head." The old man replies, "Yeah I know! That's why I need it lowered!"

A psychiatrist was conducting a group therapy session with four young mothers and their small children. "You all have obsessions," he observed. To the first mother, Mary, he said, "You are obsessed with eating. You've even named your daughter Candy." He turned to the second mom, Ann: "Your obsession is with money. Again, it manifests itself in your child's name, Penny." He turned to the third mom, Joyce: "Your obsession is alcohol. This too shows itself in your child's name, Brandy." At this point, the fourth mother, Kathy, quietly got up, took her little boy by the hand, and whispered, "Come on, Dick, this guy has no idea what he's talking about. Let's pick up Johnson and Willy from school

63

and go get dinner."

One day, Mr. Smith, the president of a large corporation, called his vice-president, Dave, into his office and said, "We're making some cutbacks, so either Jack or Barbara will have to be laid off." Dave looked at Mr. Smith and said, "Barbara is my best worker, but Jack has a wife and three kids. I don't know whom to fire." The next morning Dave waited for his employees to arrive. Barbara was the first to come in, so Dave said, "Barbara, I've got a problem. You see, I've got to lay you or Jack off and I don't know what to do?" Barbara replied, "You'd better jack off. I've got a headache."

A little boy and his grandfather are raking leaves in the yard. The little boy sees an earthworm trying to get back into its hole. He says, "Grandpa, I bet I can put that worm back in that hole." The grandfather replies, "I'll bet you five dollars you can't. It's too wiggly and limp to put back in that little hole." The little boy runs into the house and comes back out with a can of hair spray. He sprays the worm until it is straight and stiff as a board. The boy then proceeds to put the worm back into the hole. The grandfather hands the little boy five dollars, grabs the hair spray and runs into the house. Thirty minutes later, the grandfather comes back out and hands the boy another five dollars. The little boy says, "Grandpa, you already gave me five dollars." The grandfather replies, "I know. That's from your Grandma."

A man went into a pharmacy and asked to talk to a male pharmacist. The woman he was talking to said that she was the pharmacist and that she and her sister owned the store, so there were no males employed there. She then asked if there was something she could help the gentleman with. The man said, "This is embarrassing for me, but I have a permanent erection which causes me a lot of problems. I was wondering what you could give me for it?" The pharmacist said, "Just a minute, I'll go talk to my sister." When she returned, she said, "The best we can do is 1/3 ownership in the store and $3,000 a month in living expenses."

Mary and Lisa are having a conversation during their lunch break. Mary asks, "So, Lisa, how's your sex life these days?" Lisa replies, "Oh, you know. It's the usual, Social Security kind." "Social Security?" Mary asked quizzically. Lisa replies, "Yeah, you get a little each month, but it's not enough to live on."

A wife says to her friend, "Our sex life stinks." Her friend says, "Do you ever watch your husband's face when you're having sex?" She says, "Once, and I saw rage." Her friend says, "Why would he be angry during sex?" The wife says, "Because he was looking through the window at us."

A husband and wife were out playing golf. They tee off and one drive goes to the right and one drive goes to the left. The wife finds her ball in a patch of buttercups. She grabs a club and takes a mighty swing at the ball. She hits a beautiful second shot, but in the process she hacks and kills all of the buttercups. Suddenly a magical woman appears out of nowhere in a swirling cloud of dust. She blocks her path to her golf bag and looks at her and says, "I'm Mother Nature, and I don't like the way you treated my buttercups. From now on, you won't be able to stand the taste of butter. Each time you eat butter you will become physically ill to the point of total nausea." The mystery woman then disappears in a cloud of dust as quickly as she appeared. Shaken, the wife calls out to her husband, "Hey, where's your ball?" He replies, "It's over here in the pussy willows." The wife screams back, "DON'T HIT THE BALL! DON'T HIT THE BALL!"

A 21-year-old finally had the opportunity to go to a party by herself. Since she was very good-looking, she was a bit nervous about what to do if boys hit on her. Her mom said, "It's very easy! Whenever a boy starts hitting on you, you ask him, 'What will be the name of our baby?' That'll scare them off." So off she went. After a little while at the party, a boy started dancing with her, and little by little he started kissing her and touching her. She asked him, "What will our baby be called?" The boy found some excuse and disappeared. Soon, the same thing happened again: a boy started to kiss her neck and her shoulders. She stopped him and asked about the baby's name, and he ran off. Later on, another boy invited her for a walk. After a few minutes, he started kissing her, and she asked him, "What will our baby be called?" He continued, now slowly taking her clothes off. "What will our baby be called?" she asked once more. He began to have sex with her. "What will our baby be called?!" she asked again. After he was done, he took off his condom, gave it a knot, and said, "If he gets out of this one... David Copperfield!"

A man went into a store and began looking around. He saw a washer and dryer, but there was no price listed on them. He asked the salesperson, "How much are the washer and dryer?" "Five dollars for both of them," the salesman said. "Yeah right, you've got to be kidding me!" the man replied sarcastically. "No, that's the price," the salesman said, "Do you want to buy them or not?" "Yeah, I'll take them!" the customer responded. He continued to look around and saw a car stereo system with top-of-the-line features and accessories. "How much?" he asked. "Five dollars for the system," the salesman answered. "Is it stolen?" the guy asks. "No," said the salesman, "It's brand new, do you want it or not?" "Sure!" the customer replied. He looked around some more. Next he found a just-released computer tablet. "How much?" "Five dollars," was the familiar response. "I'll take that too!" the man said. As the salesperson is ringing up the purchases, the man asked him, "Why are your prices so cheap?" The salesman said, "Well, the owner of the store is at my house right now with my wife. What he's doing to her, I'm doing to his business!"

A couple, both age 78, went to a sex therapist's office. The doctor asked, "What can I do for you?" The man said, "Will you watch us have sexual intercourse?" The doctor looked puzzled, but agreed. When the couple finished, the doctor said, "There's nothing wrong with the way you have intercourse," and he charged them $50. This happened several weeks in a row. The couple would make an appointment, have intercourse with no problems, pay the doctor, then leave. Finally, the doctor asked, "Just exactly what are you trying to find out?" The old man said, "We're not trying to find out anything. She's married and we can't go to her house. I'm married and we can't go to my house. The Holiday Inn charges $90. The Hilton charges $108. We do it here for $50, and I get $43 back from Medicare."

Three sisters wanted to get married, but their parents couldn't afford three services, so they had all of them get married on the same day. They also couldn't afford to send all three couples on a honeymoon, so all three daughters stayed at home for their wedding night with their husbands. That night, the mother got up because she couldn't sleep. When she went past her oldest daughter's room she heard screaming. Then she went to her second daughter's room and she heard laughing. Then she went to her youngest daughter's room and she couldn't hear anything. The next morning, when the men left, the mother asked her oldest daughter, "Why were you screaming last night?" The daughter replied, "Mom you always told me if something hurt I should scream." The mother replied, "That's true." She looked at her second daughter. "Why were you laughing so much last night?" The daughter replied, "Mom you always said that if something tickled you should laugh." The mother replied, "That's also true." Then the mother looked at her youngest daughter. "Why was it so quiet in your room last night?" The youngest daughter replied, "Mom, you always told me I should never talk with my mouth full."

A couple was invited to a swanky masked Halloween party. The wife got a terrible headache and told her husband to go to the party alone. He, being a devoted husband, protested, but she argued and said she was going to take some aspirin and go to bed, and there was no need for him to stay home. So he took his costume and away he went. The wife, after sleeping soundly for one hour, awakened without pain. As it was still early, she decided to go to the party. Since her husband did not know what her costume was, she thought she would have some fun by watching her husband to see how he acted when she was not with him. She joined the party and soon spotted her husband on the dance floor, dancing with every attractive woman he could and copping a little feel here and a little kiss there. His wife up to him and started to dance sensually with him. She let him go as far as he wished; naturally, since he was her husband. Finally, he whispered a little proposition in her ear and she agreed, so off they went to one of the cars and had a little fling. Just before unmasking at midnight, she slipped away and went home. She put the costume away and got into bed, wondering what kind of explanation he would make for his behavior. She was sitting up reading when he came in. She asked what kind of a time he had. He said, "Oh the same old thing. You know I never have a good time when you're not there." The she asked, "Did you dance much?" He replied, "I'll tell you, I never even danced one dance. When I got there, I met some of my friends, so we went into the den and played poker all evening. But I'll tell you- the guy I loaned my costume to sure had a really good time!"

An older man goes to the doctor asking for a prescription for Viagra. The man asks for a large dose of the strongest variety. The doctor asks why he needs so much. The man says that two young nymphomaniacs are spending a week at his place. The doctor fills the prescription. Later that week, the same guy goes back to the doctor asking for pain killers. The doctor asks, "Why, is your dick in that much pain?" "No," says the man. "It's for my wrists - the girls never showed up!"

# Race, Ethnicity, and Religion Jokes

Why do Jewish men get circumcised?  Because Jewish women won't touch anything unless it's 20 percent off.

Why can't Jesus eat M&Ms?  Because they keep falling through the holes in his hand.

What's the difference between a Catholic wife and a Jewish wife?  A Catholic wife has real orgasms and fake jewelry.

The cannibals ate the missionary to get a taste of religion, but they felt sick afterwards because it's hard to keep a good man down.

Religion is like a penis: it's good to have one and it's good to be proud of it, but the problem starts when you begin flaunting it in public.

How was copper wire invented?  Two Jews pulling on a penny.

God runs into Adam in the Garden of Eden and asks if he's seen Eve around. Adam says they just finished making love and she's down by the river washing up. The skies darken, thunder booms as lighting races across the sky and God screams "NO!" Adam cowers in fear and asks why the Lord is displeased. God cries,

"How am I ever going to get that smell out of the fish?"

Did you hear about the new Jewish sports car? It can turn on a dime- and pick it up too.

A Catholic couple is about to get married, and the woman sits the man down for a heart-to-heart the day before the wedding. She says, "Honey, before we do this, I have something I need to get off my chest. You see, a few years back, my family was very poor, and for a while I had to work as a prostitute." The man leaps out of his chair and shouts, "Oh no, absolutely not! I can't get married to you!" The woman starts crying, and begs him to forgive her, "Please don't leave me - surely you can live with a woman who used to be a bit of a whore..." The man sits down and says, "Oh, that's fine. For a minute I thought you said *Protestant*."

What happens when a Jew has a boner and runs straight towards a wall? He breaks his nose.

Jesus walks into a hotel. He hands the innkeeper three nails, and says, "Can you put me up for the night?"

How is God just like a regular man? If you're not on your knees, he's not interested.

Does a rabbi get paid for circumcision or does he just keep the tips?

Ruth and Golda were walking along Hendon High Street. Ruth says, "My son Irving is getting married. He tells me he is engaged to a wonderful girl, but... he thinks she may have a disease called herpes." Golda says, "Do you have any idea what this herpes is, and can he catch it?" Ruth replies, "No, but I am just so thrilled to hear about Irving's engagement - it's time he settled down. As far as the herpes goes...who knows?" "Well," says Golda, "I have a very good medical dictionary at home. I'll look it up and call you." So Golda goes home, looks it up, and calls Ruth. "Ruth, I found it. Not to worry. It says herpes is a disease of the gentiles."

Why did God create orgasms? So women can moan even when they're happy.

The children were gathered on the front pew one Sunday morning for the Children's Sermon. The minister asked, "Does anyone know what the resurrection is?" One boy blurted out, "I'm not quite sure but I do know that if you have a resurrection that lasts longer than four hours, you have to see a doctor."

A woman has a sip of wine. She tastes it, and then has another longer sip. She says to the man who gave her the cup, "Oooh yes- I like it. I'll have a bottle of this please." The priest responds, "Ma'am, that's now how this works! Go back to your church pew."

Three Italian nuns die and go to heaven. At the Pearly Gates, they are met by St. Peter. He says "Sisters, you all led such wonderful lives that I'm granting you six months to go back to earth and be anyone you want to be." The first nun says, "I want to be Sophia Loren," and *poof* she's gone. The second says, "I want to be Madonna," and *poof* she's gone. The third says, "I want to be Sara Pipalini." St. Peter looks perplexed. "Who?" he says. "Sara Pipalini," replies the nun. St. Peter shakes his head and says, "I'm sorry, but that name just doesn't ring a bell." The nun then takes a newspaper out of her habit and hands it to St. Peter. He reads the paper and starts laughing. He hands it back to her and says, "No sister, the paper says it was the 'Sahara Pipeline' that was laid by 1,400 men in six months."

What's black and screams? Stevie Wonder answering the iron.

Why do the Scottish men wear kilts? Because a sheep can hear a zipper from like a mile away.

What's the difference between a northern fairytale and a

southern fairytale? A northern fairytale begins "Once upon a time ..." A southern fairytale begins "Y'all ain't gonna believe this shit..."

What's the Cuban National Anthem? Row, Row, Row Your Boat.

Watching Olympic track running makes you feel like you witnessed a crime. You hear a gunshot and then see a bunch of black guys hauling ass.

What do you get when you cross a Mexican and a black man? Someone who is too lazy to steal.

An American, a Chinese man, and a Mexican are all on an airplane. The plane is going down because it's been overloaded. The Chinese guy throws rice off the plane, saying, "I have enough of this back in my country." The Mexican throws beans off the plane, saying, "I have enough of these in my country. The American throws the Mexican out of the plane, saying, "I have enough of these in my country."

Why can't you play Uno with a Mexican? They steal all the green cards.

Why doesn't Mexico have an Olympic team? Because everybody who can run, jump and swim are already in the United States.

What would Martin Luther King be if he was white? Alive.

What did the little Mexican boy get for Christmas? My bike.

A black guy and a Mexican guy opened a restaurant. It's called "Nacho Daddy."

Hey, I'm not saying Hitler was a great guy, but he really saved the History channel.

What did Davey Crockett say at the Alamo? "Where did all these landscapers come from?"

What did God say when he made the third black person? "Damn I burned another one!"

How come there aren't any Mexicans on Star Trek? They don't work in the future either.

# Dirty Pickup Lines

There are a lot of fish in the sea, but you're the only one I'd like to catch and mount back home.

Do you want to see a magic trick? Watch me pull something out of my pants!

I like my woman how I like my glasses- sitting on my face.

Do you sell hot dogs? Because you know how to make a wiener stand.

If your left leg was Thanksgiving, and your right leg is Christmas, can I come visit you between the holidays?

Fuck me if I'm wrong, but isn't your name Cindrella?

My dick just died.  Can I bury it in your vagina?

Wanna go on an ate with me? I'll give you the D later.

Are you a termite? Cause you're about to have a mouth full of wood.

There are so many things you can do with the mouth- why waste it on talking?

Your ass is pretty tight, want me to loosen it up?

I'm like Domino's Pizza. If I don't cum in 30 minutes, the next one is free.

Are you an architect, because I want you on staff for my next erection.

Are you fertilizer, because you just made me grow six inches.

This dick a rental car company. It Hertz.

How about later tonight, you let me slip into something a little more comfortable... Like your vagina.

Do you like cherries? If not can I have yours?

I'd treat you like a snow storm- I'll give you six to eight inches and make it mildly inconvenient for you to move in the morning.

My cat's dead, can I play with your pussy instead?

Hey baby, I'm kind of cold. Can I use your thighs as earmuffs?

Hey! tell your nipples to stop staring at my eyes.

Some men go around telling women they have an eight-inch penis; I'd never shortchange myself like that!

I'm bigger and better than the Titanic. Only 200 woman went down on the Titanic.

Why pay five dollars when you can get this footling for free.

I know why they call it a beaver- it's dying for some wood.

I'm a hard worker. Do you have an opening I can fill?

You know what would make my face look better? If you sat on it.

I heard you weren't feeling well. Do you need a shot of penis-ilin?

Are you a tortilla? Because I want to flip you over and eat you out!

There are eight planets in the universe, but only seven after I destroy Uranus.

I must be hunting treasure because I'm digging your chest.

Do you believe in karma? Because I know some good karma-sutra positions.

I might not go down in history, but I'll go down on you!

I'm no weatherman, but you can expect a few inches tonight.

I like every bone in your body, especially mine.

You know what I like in a girl? My dick.

You know why they call me the cat whisperer? Cause I know exactly what that pussy needs.

The socks are having a party; can the pants come down?

You know how some men buy really expensive cars to make up for certain shortages? Well, I don't even own a car.

Would you like to try an Australian kiss? It is just like a French kiss, but down under.

You are so selfish! You're going to have that body the rest of your life and I just want it for one night.

What time do you get off? Can I watch?

The only reason I would kick you out of bed would be to fuck you on the floor.

The only thing I want between our relationship is latex.

Wanna play Army? I lay down and you blow the hell outta me.

Since we've been told to reduce waste these days, what do you say we use these condoms in my pocket before they expire.

# Gay Jokes

How can you make a gay man scream twice? After sex, wash your hands and dry them with the curtains.

What's the best part of sex with a transvestite? Reaching around and pretending it went all the way through.

What do you call a homosexual in a wheelchair? Rolaids.

Where do lesbians store their alcohol? In a lick-er cabinet.

A deer walks out of a gay bar and exclaims, "Damn I just blew 30 bucks in there."

Have you heard about the guy who discovered that he's both dyslexic and gay? He's still in Daniel!

What does a gay man and an ambulance have in common? They both get loaded from the rear.

What comes after 69 for gay men? Mouthwash.

What did one gay sperm say to another? "How do we find an egg in all of this shit?"

My dyslexic gay friend is so excited for February 14th. He thinks it's Vaseline Day!

What do you call a person who pays for sex with both men and women? A buysexual.

What do you call lesbian twins? Lick-a-likes.

Did you know 75 percent of the gay population were born that way? The other 25 percent were sucked into it.

How do you turn a fruit into a vegetable? AIDS.

Why do lesbians suck at cooking? Because they prefer to eat out.

How does a gay guy fake an orgasm? He spits on his partner's back.

I met a lesbian who was so butch, she rolled her own tampons.

What did one lesbian vampire say to the other lesbian vampire? "I'll see you next month."

Daughter: "Day, I'm a lesbian." Dad: "Okay, but you can never bring a girlfriend home." Daughter: "Why not?" Dad: "She'd turn straight as soon as she laid her eyes on me."

A man goes to a bar and orders ten shots of whiskey. The bartender says, "Wow, that's a lot! Are you celebrating something?" The man says, "Yes! My first blowjob." The bartender says, "Congrats! Why ten shots?" The man says, "*If that won't get the taste out, nothing will.*"

What do you call a lesbian with fat fingers? Well hung.

My lesbian neighbors asked me what I wanted for my birthday. They gave me a Rolex. I think they misunderstood when I said, "I wanna watch."

What does a lesbian have in common with a mechanic? Snap-on tools!

What's the difference between a gay man and a refrigerator? The fridge doesn't fart when you pull your meat out.

How can you tell if a lesbian is butch? She kick starts her vibrator.

Two gay men were walking through a zoo. They came across the gorillas and after a while they noticed that the huge male gorilla had a massive erection. This fascinated the gay men so much they couldn't take their eyes off of it. One of the men just couldn't bear it any longer and he reached into the cage to touch it. The gorilla grabbed him, dragged him into the cage and screwed him for six hours non-stop.  When he was done, the gorilla threw the gay man back out of the cage. An ambulance was called and the man was taken away to the hospital. The next day his friend visits him in the hospital and asked, "Are you hurt?" "AM I HURT?" he shouted, "Wouldn't you be? That big ape hasn't called, he hasn't written..."

An obnoxious drunk in a bar keeps hitting on a lesbian who is waiting for her date. The drunk just won't take no for an answer. "Tell you what, I'll sleep with you if you can name one thing a man can do for me that my dildo can't!" the lesbian says. The obnoxious drunk thinks for a moment, and says, "Okay, let's see your dildo buy the next round of drinks!"

A gay guy walks into the doctor's office. He takes off his clothes for examination. When he takes his clothes off, the doctor sees a Nicoderm patch at the end of his penis. The doctor says, "Hmmm, that's interesting.  Does it work?" The gay man answers, "Sure does!  haven't had a butt in three weeks!"

Three middle-aged men were golfing together. All three were proud parents, and they were bragging about their children.  "My son is doing incredibly well for himself," the first man says. "He's a lawyer, and he's just rolling in the money! In fact, he has so much money that he bought his friend a sports car." The second man says, "I can top that. My son is even wealthier! He's a skilled brain surgeon; he makes a fortune. He has so much money that he bought his friend a huge house." "What about you, George?" the two men ask their friend. George sheepishly looked at his feet. "Well, my son is, um … well, he's in gay porn." His two friends expressed their condolences. Then, George said: "Still, I guess he's doing well for himself. After all, he has a huge house and drives a brand-new sports car."

Did you hear about the gay security guard who got fired from his job at the sperm bank? He got caught drinking on the job.

Did you hear about the two gay guys that had an argument in the bar? They went outside to exchange blows.

Did you hear about the gay truckers? They exchanged loads.

What's the biggest crime committed by transvestites? Male fraud.

# Insult Jokes

Save your breath... You'll need it to blow up your date.

You have the right to remain silent because whatever you say will probably be stupid anyway.

You still use Internet Explorer? You must like it nice and slow.

Yo' mamma is like a vacuum cleaner- she sucks, blows, and gets laid in the closet.

The only way you'll ever get laid is if you crawl up a chicken's ass and wait.

You're not the sharpest tool in the shed, but you're the biggest.

If you really want to know about mistakes, you should ask your parents.

If bullshit could float, you'd be the admiral of the fleet.

If I had a face like yours, I'd sue my parents.

Makeup tip: You're not in the circus.

I don't think you act stupid. I'm sure it's the real thing.

Roses are red, violets are blue, God made me pretty, what happened to you?

Which sexual position produces the ugliest children? Ask your mother.

I wasn't born with enough middle fingers to let you know how I feel about you.

It looks like your face caught on fire and someone tried to put it out with a hammer.

If I wanted to hear from an asshole, I'd fart.

You'll never be the man your mother is.

# Yeah, We Went There Jokes

Why did the necrophiliac furry quit BDSM? He realized he was beating a dead horse.

Say what you want about pedophiles... at least they slow down for school zones.

What do broccoli and sodomy have in common? If they're forced upon you as a kid, you probably won't like them when you're older.

What is the difference between acne and a catholic priest? Acne usually comes on a boy's face after he turns twelve.

What do spinach and anal sex have in common? If you were forced to have it as a kid, you'll hate it as an adult.

How do you get a nun pregnant? Dress her up as an altar boy.

My girlfriend called me a pedophile, and I said, "That's a pretty big word for a 10-year-old!"

What do Pink Floyd and Dale Earnhardt have in common? Their last big hit was the wall.

What's the difference between Hitler and Michael Phelps? Phelps can finish a race.

What do you get when you cross A-Rod with Chris Brown? A cheater, cheater, woman beater.

What do you call a school bus full of white people? Twinkie.

Did you hear about the celebrity murderer? He was shooting for the stars.

What does an 80-year-old woman taste like? Depends.

Why was the guitar teacher arrested?  For fingering a minor.

What do the Mafia and pussies have in common?  One slip of the tongue, and you're in deep shit.

A priest and rabbi are walking down the street together when a seven-year-old boy walks by. The priest turns to the rabbi and says, "Lets screw that little boy." The rabbi looks at the priest and says, "Out of what?"

When is it time to go to bed at Michael Jackson's house?  When the big hand touches the little hand.

A man and a woman are sitting at the bar one night, drinking their problems away. After a time, the man decides to ask the woman, "What's the matter, you seem really down?" The woman responds, "Well, it's just that my husband left me." The man looked surprised as the woman was quite attractive and asked "Why would he leave you?" The woman replied, "He said I was too kinky in the bedroom." Immediately the man's eyes lit up in shock at her answer. "My wife actually just left me for the same reason," he told her, and it was the truth. The two of them continue talking, and eventually she invites the man to her home. They enter her bedroom, the woman instructs the man to take a seat on the bed, and says that she is going to "get ready" in the other room. The woman proceeds to attire herself in a leather corset, complete with whip, chains, and ball gag. She heads to the pantry and grabs a bottle of whipped cream and some Tabasco sauce. The woman then reenters the bedroom to see the man putting on his coat about to walk out the door. The woman exclaims, "What's the matter? I thought you were kinky!" The man replied, "Lady, I just fucked your dog and shit in your purse, I'm done here."

Two pedophiles were walking down the street one day when they came across a pair of small lacey panties on the ground. The first one picks them up, smells them and goes, "Aahhh... A seven-year-old girl." The other grabs them from him and also takes a smell and goes, "No, no ... Definitely an eight-year-old girl!" The two of them are them smelling them in turns and arguing. "An eight-year-old!" "No, a seven-year-old!" "Definitely an eight-year-old!" .... and so on. The local priest is walking past as the two men argue and can't help but ask them what the commotion is all about. The first pedophile tells the priest, and asks him if he could sort out the argument. So the priest takes the panties, has a good long sniff, and after pondering for a few moments, he looks at the two men and says: "Definitely an eight-year-old girl! But not from my parish!"

I locked my keys in my car outside of an abortion clinic the other night. It turns out they get really pissed when you go in and ask them for a coat hanger.

An elementary school teacher, a lawyer, a Catholic priest and three young boys are on a plane with only three parachutes. Engines explode, plane starts going down. The teacher screams, "Save the children!" The lawyer yells, "FUCK THE CHILDREN!" The Catholic priest looks around and whispers, "Is there time?"

What's the difference between your mom and driveways? I pull out of driveways.

What does a silver medalist and a priest have in common? They both came in a little behind.

Why does Helen Keller masturbate with one hand? So she can moan with the other.

What do priests and McDonald's have in common? They both stick their meat in 10-year-old buns.

What do an airport and an illegal abortion have in common? The Hanger.

A groom and his father are standing at the bar after the wedding in Alabama. The father says to the groom, "If I were 20 years younger she would have been mine." The groom replied, "Don't you dare talk about my sister like that!"

What do you call an incestuous nephew? An aunt-eater.

Abstinence makes the Church grow fondlers.

What's the difference between a rabbi and a priest? A rabbi cuts them off; A priest sucks them off.

A guy walks into a pub and sees a sign hanging over the bar that reads: "CHEESEBURGER: $1.50 CHICKEN SANDWICH: $2.50 HAND JOB: $20.00." He walks up to the bar and beckons one of the three exceptionally attractive blondes serving drinks. "Can I help you?" she asks. "I was wondering," whispers the man. "Are you the one who gives the hand jobs?" "Yes," she purrs. "I am." The man replies, "Well, wash your hands. I want a cheeseburger."

Ten Catholic priests were killed in a road accident. At the pearly gates, Saint Peter says, " If any of you are pedophiles you can go straight to hell!" Nine of them start to walk away when Saint Peter calls out, "And take this deaf priest with you!"

One day a single mother was in the grocery store with her four kids. They were acting up, screaming, running around, and knocking items off the shelves. The mother grabbed all of them and shouted, "I should have swallowed all of you!"

Two men are playing tennis. One man falls and hits his elbow and decides to go to an emergency clinic. The other man says, "Don't waste your money going to the hospital. Just go inside the store at the corner down the street, put $10 in the machine in the corner, piss in the cup, let it do its thing and a slip of paper will come out that tells you what you have." So he goes to the store, puts ten dollars in the machine, pisses in the cup, and out comes a piece of paper. It says: "You have tennis elbow- take this ointment cream and apply it on your elbow 3-4 times a daily." So the man goes home wondering how it know what was wrong, and wanted to see if this machine is a real miracle worker. So he goes home and gets his sister's urine, his brother's urine, and his dog's urine, and he jacks-off in the cup. He goes back to the store, puts ten dollars in the machine, and places the cup in the machine. The paper comes out and says: "Your sister has gonorrhea, your brother is gay, your dog has fleas, and if you keep jacking-off like that you'll never lose that tennis elbow."

A man travels to Spain and goes to a Madrid restaurant for a late dinner. He orders the house special and he is brought a plate with potatoes, corn, and two large meaty objects. "What's this?" he asks. "Cojones, senor," the waiter replies. "What are cojones?" the man asks. "Cojones," the waiter explains, "are the testicles of the bull who lost at the arena this afternoon." At first the man is disgusted, but being the adventurous type, he decides to try this local delicacy. To his amazement, it is quite delicious. In fact, it is so good that he decides to come back again the next night and order it again. After dinner, the man informed the waiter that these were better than the pair he had the previous afternoon but the portion was much smaller. "Senor," the waiter explains, "the bull does not lose every time."

One day, after striking gold in Alaska, a lonesome miner came down from the mountains and walked into a saloon in the nearest town. "I'm lookin' for the meanest, roughest and toughest whore in the Yukon!" he said to the bartender. "We got her!" replied the bartender. "She's upstairs in the second room on the right." The miner handed the bartender a gold nugget to pay for his time with the woman and two beers. He grabbed the beer bottles, stomped up the stairs, kicked open the second door on the right and yelled, "I'm lookin' for the meanest, roughest and toughest whore in the Yukon!" The woman inside the room looked at the miner and said, "You found her!" Then she stripped naked, bent over and grabbed her ankles. "How do you know I want to do it in that position?" asked the miner. "I don't," replied the woman, "but I thought you might like to open those beers before we get started."

A man was driving on a highway when he saw a guy tied up to a tree, crying. The man stopped his car, and walked up to the guy. "What happened?" he asked. The guy sobbed, "I was driving and picked up a hitchhiker. He pulled a gun on me, robbed me, took all my money, my clothes, my car and then tied me up." The man studied the guy for a moment, and then pulled down his pants and whipped out his dick. "I guess this isn't your lucky day, pal!"

A young teenaged girl was a prostitute and, for obvious reasons, kept it a secret from her grandma. One day, the police raided a brothel and arrested a group of prostitutes, including the young girl. The prostitutes were instructed to line up in a straight line on the sidewalk. Well, who should be walking in the neighborhood, but her grandma. The young girl was frantic. Sure enough, Grandma noticed her young granddaughter and asked curiously, "What are you lining up for, dear?" Not willing to let grandma in on her little secret, the young girl told her that some people were passing out free oranges and that she was lining up for some. "Mmm, sounds lovely," said Grandma. "I think I'll have some myself," she continued as she made her way to the back of the line. A police officer made his way down the line, questioning all of the prostitutes. When he got to Grandma, at the end of the line, he was bewildered. "But you're so old... how do you do it?" Grandma replied, "Oh, it's quite easy, sonny... I just remove my dentures and suck them dry!"

# Dark Humor Jokes

A man goes into a library and asks for a book on suicide. The librarian says, "No- you won't bring it back."

Why don't people tell jokes about Jonestown? The punch line is too long.

I was walking in a cemetery this morning and saw a man hiding behind a gravestone. I said, "Morning." He replied, "No, taking a leak."

A girl in a bar said to me, "I wouldn't fuck you if you were the last person alive." Leaning over and whispering, I replied, "But who would be around to stop me?"

What's blue and has 100 nipples? The dumpster at the cancer clinic.

A young man went up to his father and asked him, "Can I have twenty bucks for a blow job?" His father said, "I don't know. Are you any good?"

A recent survey shows that sperm banks beat blood banks in contributions, hands down.

A grieving widow went to her local newspaper to submit an obituary. The man behind the counter told her it will cost $5.00 per word. She thinks for a moment and says, "Fred's dead." The man then informs her there is a five-word minimum. She thinks and replies, "Okay... print 'Fred's dead; Buick for sale."

What's worse than waking up at a party and finding a penis drawn on your face? Finding out it was traced.

Late one night a woman was walking home when a man grabbed her and dragged her into the bushes. "Help me! Help me!" she screamed. "I'm being robbed!" "You ain't being robbed," her attacker interrupted. "You're being screwed!" The woman looked down at her attacker as he unzipped his jeans. "If you're screwing me with that," she fumed, "I am being robbed!"

My girlfriend and I were having sex the other day when she looked at me and said, "Make love to me like in the movies." So I fucked her in the ass, pulled out, and came all over her face and hair. I guess we don't watch the same movies.

To avoid being raped when I am in jail, I stick a tube of toothpaste up my ass for complete cavity protection.

Why is a man's pee yellow, and his sperm white? So he can tell if he's coming or going.

Crowded elevators smell different to midgets.

What did Helen Keller say when she put down the cheese grater? *"That's the worst book I ever read!"*

Why did Snow White get kicked out of Disneyland? She sat on Pinocchio's face and screamed, "Lie to me! Lie to me!"

A man goes to a shrink and says, "Doctor, my wife is unfaithful to me. Every evening, she goes to Larry's bar and picks up men. In fact, she sleeps with anybody who asks her! I'm going crazy. What do you think I should do?" "Relax," says the Doctor, "take a deep breath and calm down. Now, tell me, exactly where is Larry's bar?"

Breaking up with Asian girls is the worst. They don't hear it the first time, so you have to drop the bomb twice.

I'm not saying she's a slut, but her vagina should be in the NFL Hall of Fame for greatest wide-receiver.

Two homeless men are standing around bragging about their day. The first hobo says, "Today I found $20, and was able to buy a nice hot meal. It was my luckiest day ever!" The second hobo replies, "Oh yeah, my day was way better! I was at the train yard, and found a woman tied to the train tracks. After I untied her, we fucked all day long!" The first hobo asks, "Did you get a blow job?" The other replied, "No, I couldn't find her head."

A kid comes home from school, runs up to his mom and says, "Mom, I just found out that I have the biggest dick in the whole third grade! Is it because I am black?" The mom says, "No, it is probably because you are 18."

Two nuns are biking down the cobblestone streets of Rome. "I've never come this way before," one of the nuns says, quite breathlessly. The other responds, "It's the cobblestones."

A married couple down on their luck decides to make a few extra bucks by reluctantly having the wife work the corner. After the first day, the husband picks her up and asks, "How did you do?" She says, "I did pretty well, I made $200.50." He asks, "What asshole gave you 50 cents?" She replies, "All of them."

What's the difference between your mom and a washing machine? The washing machine doesn't call me for three weeks after I dump my load in it.

What is the difference between jelly and jam? I can't jelly my penis in your ass.

What's the best thing about dating homeless women? You can drop them off anywhere.

What do George Zimmerman, OJ Simpson and Masturbation have in common? Getting off once isn't enough.

What did the leper say to the prostitute? Keep the tip.

What did the cannibal do after he dumped his girlfriend? He wiped his butt.

What is the difference between an illegal immigrant and E.T.? E.T. eventually went home.

A man from Texas buys a round of drinks for everyone in the bar as he announces his wife has just produced "A typical Texas baby boy weighing twenty pounds." Congratulations were offered from all around, and many exclamations of "Wow!" were heard. Two weeks later he returns to the bar. The bartender says, "Say, you're the father of the typical Texas baby that weighed twenty pounds at birth, aren't you? How much does the baby weigh now?" The proud father answers, "Fifteen pounds." The bartender is puzzled.

"Why? What happened? He already weighed twenty pounds at birth." The Texas father takes a slow sip from his beer, wipes his lips on his shirt sleeve, leans over to the bartender and proudly announces, "Had him circumcised."

What do Princess Diana and Pink Floyd have in common?  Their last big hit was the wall.

A vampire goes into a pub and asks for boiling water. The bartender says, "I thought you only drank blood?" The vampire pulls out a used tampon and says, "I'm making tea."

What should you do if your girlfriend starts smoking?  Slow down and use a lubricant.

An elephant asked a camel, "Why are your breasts on your back?" "Well," says the camel, "I think that's a strange question from somebody whose dick is on his face."

What do a bungee jump and a hooker have in common?  They're both cheap, fast, and if the rubber breaks, you're pretty much screwed.

How is tightrope walking like getting a blowjob from someone ugly?  If you want to enjoy either, you absolutely can't look down.

A man goes to the supermarket and notices an attractive woman waving at him. She says hello. He's rather taken aback because he can't place where he knows her from. So he says, "Do you know me?" She replies, "I think you're the father of one of my kids." Now his mind travels back to the only time he has ever been unfaithful to his wife and says, "Are you the stripper from the bachelor party that I made love to on the pool table with all my buddies watching while your partner whipped my butt with wet celery?" She looks into his eyes and says calmly, "No, I'm your son's teacher."

What do you call two men fighting over a slut? Tug-of-whore.

A man went out hunting. He had all the gear, the jacket, the boots and the double-barreled shotgun. As he was climbing over a fence, he dropped the gun and it went off, right on his penis. He rushed to the hospital and was taken right into surgery. When he woke up from the operation, he found that the doctor had done a marvelous job repairing his penis. As he got ready to go home, the doctor gave him a business card. "This is my brother's card. I'll make an appointment for you to see him." The man says, "Is your brother a doctor?" "No," The doctor replies, "He plays the flute. He'll show you where to put your fingers so you don't piss in your eye."

A nerdy accountant is sent to jail for embezzlement and they put him in a cell with a huge evil looking guy. The big guy says, "I want to have some sex. You wanna be the husband or the wife?" The accountant replies, "Well, if I have to be one or the other, I guess I'd rather be the husband." The big guy says, "Okay. Now get over here and suck your wife's dick."

Why are there only two pallbearers at a homeless guy's funeral? There are only two handles on a garbage can.

An old maid wanted to travel by bus to the pet cemetery with the remains of her cat. As she boarded the bus, she whispered to the driver, "I have a dead pussy." The driver pointed to the woman in the seat behind him and said, "Sit with my wife. You two have a lot in common."

Why did Hitler commit suicide? He got the gas bill.

A woman is at the funeral of her deceased husband. Before anyone comes, during last minute checks before the viewing, she notices his corpse has a raging hard on. She panics and doesn't know what to do. She scrambles around the funeral parlor, finds a knife, and then cuts the boner off the corpse. She is now standing there with her deceased husband's penis in her hand and no clue what do with it, and her family is coming in any minute. Then it dawns on her. She drops his pants and plugs his severed dick up his ass. She leans in and says, "Good, now you know how it feels."

At the cinema a man noticed a young woman sitting all by herself. He was excited to see she had both hands under her skirt and was fingering herself furiously. He moved to the next seat to her and offered his help. She welcomed his help, and so the man started fingering her like crazy. When he tired and withdrew his hand, he was surprised to see her go back to work on herself with both hands. Wasn't I good enough?" he asked sheepishly. "Great," she said, "but these crabs are still itching!"

A doctor walked into a bank. Preparing to endorse a check, he pulled a rectal thermometer out of his shirt pocket and tried to write with it. Realizing his mistake, he looked at the thermometer with annoyance and said, "Well that's great, just great... some asshole's got my pen."

Doctor: "Your wife either has Alzheimer's or AIDS." Husband: "How can we find out which?" Doctor: "I need you to run a little experiment this weekend. Take your wife to a park and leave her there. If she finds her way home; don't fuck her."

A waitress walks up to one of her tables in a New York City restaurant and notices that the three Japanese businessmen seated there are furiously masturbating. She says, "What the hell do you guys think you are doing?" One of the Japanese men says, "Can't you see? We are all very hungry." The waitress says, "So how is whacking-off in the middle of the restaurant going to help that situation?" One of the other businessmen replies: "The menu say- FIRST COME, FIRST SERVED!"

After discovering her young daughter playing doctor with the neighbor's son, the angry mother grabbed the boy by the ear and dragged him to his house to confront his mother. The boy's mother said, "It's only natural for young boys and girls to explore their sexuality by playing doctor at their age." "Sexuality my ass!" The mother yelled. "He took out her appendix!"

A wealthy couple prepared to go out for the evening. The woman of the house gave their butler, Jervis, the night off. She said they would return home very late, and she hoped he would enjoy his evening. The wife wasn't having a good time at the party. So, she came home early, alone. Her husband stayed on, socializing with important clients. As the woman walked into her house, she found Jervis by himself in the dining room. She called him to follow her, and led him into the master bedroom. She turned to him and said, in the voice she knew he must obey, "Jervis, I want you to take off my dress." This he did, hanging it carefully over a chair. "Jervis," she continued, "now take off my stockings and garter belt." Again, Jervis silently obeyed. "Now, Jervis, I want you to remove my bra and panties." Eyes downcast, Jervis obeyed. Both were breathing heavily, the tension mounting between them. She looked sternly at him and said, "Jervis, if I ever catch you wearing my stuff again, you're fired!"

What does a cannibal get when he comes home late for dinner? A cold shoulder.

A homeless man walks by a new bar that is opening up in town. The bar is having a "name the bar" contest and the man says, "What about calling the bar 'Lucy's Legs?'" The bar owners love the name and tell the man he won. The prize is a year of free food and drink at the bar, and they tell the man to come back the next morning. The next day, the man is sitting on the ground outside of the bar, waiting for them to open. A cop comes by and says, "Hey, what are you doing here?" The man responds, "I'm waiting for Lucy's Legs to open so I can get a drink!"

What did the maxi pad say to the fart? "You're the wind beneath
109

my wings."

An elderly man goes into his doctor's office for an annual physical. After a while, the doctor comes out and says, "I'm sorry Bill, but we have discovered you have a condition which only allows you another six weeks to live."   "But Doctor," Bill replied, "I feel great. I haven't felt better in years. This just can't be true. Isn't there anything I can do?"   After a moment the doctor said, "Well, you might start going down the street to that new health spa and take a mud bath every day."   Excitedly Bill asked, "And that will cure me?"   "No," replied the doctor, "but it will get you used to the dirt."

A man is at his doctor's office for his annual exam.  "Doctor," the man says, "I want to be castrated."   "What on earth for?" asks the doctor in amazement.  The man answers, "It's something I've been thinking about for a long time and I want to have it done." The doctor is still shocked.   "But have you thought it through properly?" asks the doctor. "It's a very serious operation and once it's done, there's no going back. It will change your life forever!" The man replies, "I'm aware of that and you're not going to change my mind -- either you book me in to be castrated or I'll simply go to another doctor." "Well, okay," says the doctor, "But it's against my recommendation!"  So the man has his operation, and the next day he is up and walking very slowly, legs apart, down the hospital corridor with his IV drip stand. Heading towards him is another patient, who is walking exactly the same way. "Hi there," says the man, "It looks as if you've just had the same operation as me." "Well," said the patient, "I finally decided after 37 years of life that I would like to be circumcised." The man paused, stared at him in horror, and screamed, "Shit! THAT'S the word!"

A trucker goes into a whorehouse and hands the madam five hundred dollars. He says, "I want your ugliest woman and a bologna sandwich." The madam says, "For that kind of money, you could have one of my finest girls and surf and turf." The trucker says, "I'm not horny, I'm homesick."

A man calls his boss, but the boss' wife answers the phone instead. "I'm afraid he died last week," she explains. The next day the man calls again and asks for the boss. "I told you," the wife replies, "he died last week." The next day he calls again and once more asks to speak to his boss. By this time the wife is getting upset and shouts, "I've already told you that my husband, your boss, is dead. Why do keep calling?" "Because," he replied laughing, "I just love hearing it!"

An old lady in a nursing home is wheeling up and down the halls in her wheelchair making sounds like she's driving a car. As she's going down the hall an old man jumps out of a room and says, "Excuse me ma'am, but you were speeding. Can I see your driver's license?" She digs around in her purse a little, pulls out a candy wrapper, and hands it to him. He looks it over, gives her a warning and sends her on her way. Up and down the halls she goes again. Again, the same old man jumps out of a room and says, "Excuse me ma'am, but I saw you cross the center line back there. Can I see your registration please?" She digs around in her purse a little, pulls out a store receipt and hands it to him. He looks it over, gives her another warning and sends her on her way. She zooms off again up and down the halls weaving all over. As she comes to the old man's room again he jumps out. This time, he's stark naked and has an erection! The old lady in the wheel chair looks up and says, "Oh no- not the Breathalyzer again!"

Two high school sweethearts who went out together for four years were both virgins. They enjoyed losing their virginity with each other in their senior year. When they graduated, they wanted to both go to the same college, but the girl was accepted to a college on the east coast, and the guy went to the west coast. They agreed to be faithful to each other and spend any time they could together. As time went on, the guy would call the girl and she would never be home, and when he wrote, she would take weeks to return the letters. Even when he emailed her, she took days to return his messages. Finally, she confessed to him she wanted to date around. He didn't take this very well and increased his calls, letters, and emails trying to win back her love. Because she became annoyed, and now had a new boyfriend, she wanted to get him off her back. So, she took a Polaroid picture of her sucking her new boyfriend's cock and sent it to her old boyfriend with a note reading, "I found a new boyfriend, leave me alone." The guy was heartbroken but, even more so, was pissed. So, he wrote on the back of the photo- "Dear Mom and Dad, having a great time at college, please send more money!" and mailed the picture to her parents.

An escaped convict broke into a house and tied up a young couple who had been sleeping in the bedroom. As soon as he had a chance, the husband turned to his voluptuous young wife, bound up on the bed in a skimpy nightgown, and whispered, "Honey, this guy hasn't seen a woman in years. Just cooperate with anything he wants. If he wants to have sex with you, just go along with it and pretend you like it. Our lives depend on it." "'Dear," the wife hissed, "I'm so relieved you feel that way, because he just told me he thinks you have a really nice, tight-looking ass!"

In a tiny village lived an old maid. In spite of her old age, she was still a virgin. She was very proud of it. She knew her last days were getting closer, so she told the local undertaker that she wanted the following inscription on her tombstone: "Born a virgin, lived a virgin, died a virgin." Not long after, the old maid died peacefully, and the undertaker told his men what the lady had said. The men went to carve it in, but they realized the inscription was too long and wouldn't fit on the tombstone. Instead, they simply wrote: "Returned unopened."

Fred had been a faithful Christian and was in the hospital, near death. The family called their pastor to stand with them. As the pastor stood next to the bed, Fred's condition appeared to deteriorate and he motioned frantically for something to write on. The pastor lovingly handed him a pen and a piece of paper, and Fred used his last bit of energy to scribble a note before he died. The pastor thought it best not to look at the note at that time, so he placed it in his jacket pocket. At the funeral, as the pastor was finishing his sermon, he realized that he was wearing the same jacket that he was wearing when Fred died. He said, "You know, Fred handed me a note just before he died. I haven't looked at it, but knowing Fred, I'm sure there's a word of inspiration there for us all." He opened the note, and read, "You're standing on my oxygen tube!"

One Fall day, Bill was out raking leaves when he noticed a hearse slowly drive by. Following the first hearse was a second hearse, which was followed by a man walking solemnly along, followed by a dog, and then about 200 men walking in single file. Intrigued, Bill went up to the man following the second hearse and asked him who was in the first hearse. "My wife," the man replied. "I'm sorry," said Bill. "What happened to her?" "My dog bit her and she died." Bill then asked the man who was in the second hearse. The man replied, "My mother-in-law. My dog bit her and she died as well." Bill thought about this for a while. He finally asked the man, "Can I borrow your dog?" The man replied, "Get in line."

Cinderella wanted to go to the ball one night, but she didn't have any tampons to use and she had her period. Her Fairy Godmother came to the rescue and turned a pumpkin next to Cinderella's house into a tampon. The Godmother said, "Now use the tampon, but be sure to get back home before midnight or it will turn back into a pumpkin!" Cinderella agreed and left the house. Midnight came along, and Cinderella had not returned yet. Hour after hour passed with no sign of her. Finally, at 5 am, Cinderella waltzed through the door. The Fairy Godmother jumped up and screamed, "Where the hell have you been?" Cinderella replied, "I met this amazing guy, and well, before I knew it, he was going after me! His name was Peter Peter something..."

A beautiful woman walks into a doctor's office one day. He is mesmerized by her beauty, and his professionalism waivers. He tells her to take her pants, she does, and he starts rubbing her thighs. "Do you know what I am doing?" asks the doctor. "Yes, checking for abnormalities," she replies. He tells her to take off her shirt and bra, she takes them off. The doctor begins rubbing her breasts and asks, "Do you know what I am doing now?" She replies, "Yes, checking for cancer." Finally, he tells her to take off her panties, lays her on the table, gets on top of her and starts having sex with her. He says to her, "Do you know what I am doing now?" She replies, "Yes, getting an STD. That's why I am here!"

A man tells his wife that he's going out to buy cigarettes. When he gets to the store he finds out it's closed. So he ends up going to the local bar to use the vending machine. While he is there, he has a few beers and begins talking to this beautiful woman. He has a few more beers, and the next thing he knows he's in the woman's apartment and they are making out. He looks up at a clock and sees that it is 2:00 am. "Oh my, god, my wife is going to kill me!" he exclaims. "Quick give me some talcum powder!" She gets him some and he rubs it all over his hands. When he gets home, his wife is up waiting for him and she's furious. "Where the hell have you been!" She screams. He says, "Well to tell you the truth, I went into a bar, had a few drinks, went home with this blonde and I slept with her." "Let me see your hands!" she demands. He shows his wife his powdery hands. "Damn liar, you were out bowling again!"

An elderly man and his wife walk into a hospital. The doctor says to the old man, "I'll need a urine sample, a feces sample, and a blood sample." The old man, who has trouble hearing, says, "What?" So the doctor says it again. Once again the old man says, "What?" With that, the old woman turns to the old man and says, "He says he needs a pair of your underwear!"

A man walks up to the bar, and speaks to the bartender. "I bet you $500 that I can piss in this cup from across the room." The bartender looks at the man like he is crazy and says with a laugh, "Ok buddy. You got a deal." So the man walks over to the other side of the room, pulls down his zipper and just lets it fly. Piss goes everywhere; on the bar, all over the bartender, but not a drop lands in the cup. The man walks back over to the bartender. The bartender says, "Ha ha ha. Well pay up." So the man pays him, turns around, and begins to laugh hysterically. The bartender asks, "You just lost $500, why are you laughing?" The man turns around and says to the bartender, "Well you see that man over there?" The man points to another man who is now slapping his hand ahead his forehead. The bartender says, "Yeah." He replies, "Well, I bet him $10,000 that I could piss all over your bar and you, and that you would be happy and laugh about it!"

A farmer hires a college student one summer to help around the farm. At the end of the summer the farmer says, "Son, since you have done such a fine job here this summer, I am going to throw a party for you." The college student says, "Wow, thank you!" The farmer says, "Well you better be able to handle a few beers because there will be lots of drinking going on." The college student says, "Hey, I can drink just as much as anyone else so I should do just fine." The farmer says, "There is also going to be a lot of fighting so I hope you are ready." The college student says, "I have been working hard all summer and I think I am in pretty good shape." The farmer says, "Well, did I mention that there will be lots of sex?" The college student says, "Good. I have been out here all summer and I have been dying for some action. What should I wear to this party?" The farmer says, "I don't care- it's just going to be me and you."

A man has a 25-inch dick. He goes to a witch in the woods and asks her if she can make his dick smaller since he just can't please the ladies because his dick is just too big. He hasn't found a lady yet who likes it and he can't get any sex. She tells him to go into the woods and he will find a magical frog. When he finds this frog, he has to ask it to marry him. If the frog says no, his cock will shrink five inches. He goes into the woods and finds this frog. He asks, "Frog, will you marry me?" The frog says "No," and his dick shrinks five inches. The guy thinks to himself, "Wow, that was pretty cool. But, it's still too big." So he goes back to the frog and again asks the frog: "Frog, will you marry me?" The frog replies: "No, I won't marry you." The guy's dick shrinks another five inches. But that's still 15 inches and he think it's still just a little bit too big. He thinks that 10 inches would be just great. He goes back to the frog and asks: "Frog, will you marry me?" The frog replies: "How many times do I have to tell you. NO, NO, NO!"

Two men were just about to tee off at the first hole of their local golf course when a man carrying a golf bag called out to them, "Do you mind if I join you? My partner didn't turn up." "Sure," they said, "You're welcome to join us." So they started playing and enjoyed the game and the company of the newcomer. Part way around the course, one of the friends asked the newcomer, "What

119

do you do for a living?" "I'm a hit man," was the reply. "You're joking!" was the response. "No, I'm not," he said, reaching into his golf bag, and pulling out a sniper's rifle with a large telescopic sight. "Here are my tools." "That's a beautiful telescopic sight," said the other friend, "Can I take a look? I think I might be able to see my house from here." So he picked up the rifle and looked through the sight in the direction of his house. "Yeah, I can see my house all right. This sight is fantastic. I can see right in the window. Wow, I can see my wife in the bedroom. Ha Ha, I can see she's naked! What's that? Wait a minute, that's my neighbor in there with her. He's naked as well! The bitch!" He turned to the hit man, "How much do you charge for a hit?" "I do a flat rate. For you, one thousand dollars every time I pull the trigger." "Can you do two for me now?" "Sure, what do you want?" "First, shoot my wife, she's always been mouthy, so shoot her in the mouth. Then the neighbor- shoot his dick off to teach him a lesson." The hit man took the rifle and took aim, standing perfectly still for a few minutes. "Are you going to do it or not?" said the friend impatiently. "Just wait a moment, be patient," said the hit man calmly, "I think I can save you a thousand dollars here..."

Did you hear about the cannibal who was expelled from school? He was buttering up his teacher.

I have the heart of a lion and a lifetime ban from the San Diego Zoo.

I have an EpiPen. My friend gave it to me when he was dying- it seemed very important to him that I have it.

# Story Jokes

A penguin sees the check engine line come on in his car, and he takes his car to the repair shop. The repairman says he can look at it but it will be a bit. The penguin walks across street, has an ice cream, and comes back to the repair shop an hour or so later. The repairman says, "It looks like you blew a seal!" The penguin says, "No, I just had some ice cream!"

A man goes to a doctor and says, "Doc, you've got to help me. My penis is orange!" The doctor examines the man and says, "You need to stop eating Cheetos while you watch porn."

A family is driving behind a garbage truck when a dildo flies out and thumps against the windscreen. Embarrassed, hoping to spare her young daughter's innocence, the mother turns around and says, "Don't worry; that was an insect." Her daughter replies, "I'm surprised it could get off the ground with a cock like that."

Two women were having lunch together, and were discussing the merits of cosmetic surgery. The first woman says, "I need to be honest with you, I'm getting a boob job." The second woman says, "Oh that's nothing, I'm thinking of having my asshole bleached!" The first woman replies, "Whoa- I just can't picture your husband as a blonde!"

An old Indian was asked the name of his wife. He replied, "Wife Name - Three Horse." "That's an unusual name for your wife, Three Horse. What does it mean?" The Indian said, "It's an old Indian name. Means Nag, Nag, Nag."

A man gets up one morning to find his wife in the kitchen, cooking. He sees one of his socks in the frying pan. "What are you doing?" he asks. "I'm doing what you asked me to do last night when you came to bed drunk," she replied. Puzzled, the man walks away thinking to himself, "I don't remember asking her to cook my sock."

A woman posts an ad in the newspaper that looks like this: "Looking for man with these qualifications- won't beat me up or run away from me, and is great in bed." She got lots of phone calls replying to her ad, but met someone perfect at her door one day. The man she met said, "Hi, I'm Bob. I have no arms so I won't beat you up, and no legs so I won't run away." The lady replies, "What makes you think you are great in bed?" Bob replies, "I rang the doorbell, didn't I?"

Three guys go to a ski lodge, and there aren't enough rooms, so they have to share a bed. In the middle of the night, the guy on the right wakes up and says, "I had this wild, vivid dream of getting a hand job!" The guy on the left wakes up, and unbelievably, he's had the same dream, too. Then the guy in the middle wakes up and says, "That's funny, I dreamed I was skiing!"

Four Catholic men and a Catholic woman were having coffee. The first Catholic man tells his friends, "My son is a priest. When he walks into a room, everyone calls him 'Father." The second Catholic man chirps, "My son is a Bishop. When he walks into a room people call him 'Your Grace." The third Catholic man says, "My son is a Cardinal. When he enters a room everyone says 'Your Eminence." The fourth Catholic man then says, "My son is the Pope. When he walks into a room people call him 'Your Holiness." Since the lone Catholic woman was sipping her coffee in silence, the four men give her a subtle look. She proudly states, "I have a daughter, slim, tall, 38D breast, 24-inch waist and 34-inch hips. When she walks into a room, people say, 'Oh My God."

An 85-year-old man was requested by his doctor for a sperm count as part of his physical exam. The doctor gave the man a jar and said, "Take this jar home and bring back a semen sample tomorrow." The next day the 85-year-old man reappeared at the doctor's office and gave him the jar, which was as clean and empty as on the previous day. The doctor asked what happened, and the man explained. "Well, doc, it's like this--first I tried with my right hand, but nothing. Then I tried with my left hand, but still nothing. Then I asked my wife for help. She tried with her right hand, then with her left, still nothing. She tried with her mouth, first with the teeth in, then with her teeth out, still nothing. We even called up the lady that lives next door and she tried too, first with both hands, then an armpit, and she even tried squeezing it between her knees, but still nothing." The doctor was shocked! He said, "You asked your neighbor?" The old man replied, "Yes, and none of us could get the jar open."

A woman is pregnant with triplets. During a mugging, she was shot three time and one bullet hit each baby. She was rushed to hospital, and was told by the miracles of science her children will survive. The doctor said the bullets would harmlessly make their way out of the kids' bodies as they grew older. The woman had two healthy girls and a healthy boy. Sixteen years later, the mother is downstairs in the living room. The first daughter comes running down the stairs. The daughter screams: "Mom, I took a piss and a bullet came out!" The mother replies: "It's okay, I knew this was going to happen one day." So she explains the story and off the daughter went. A few hours later, the second daughter came running down the stairs. She screamed: "Mom! I took a piss and a bullet came out!" The mother replied, "It's okay. I knew this was going to happen one day," and then she explains the story to the second daughter. Several hours later, the son comes running down the stairs and screams, "Mom! Mom!" The mother stops him: "I know I know- you took a piss and a bullet came out." The son screams, "No mom, I was jerking off and I shot the cat!"

A teenage girl was getting intimate with her boyfriend at her dad's house. Her father, after being woken by the noises, goes upstairs to check it out and walks in on them. "Dad!" she exclaimed in a panic. "I'm sorry!" The dad- being a dad- replies, "Hi sorry, I'm Dad!" He then turns to the boyfriend and asks, "Are you fucking sorry?"

Superman is horny as hell. He's flying around Metropolis and he spots Wonder Woman sunbathing on the roof naked with her legs spread wide open. Superman figures that he can swoop down and fuck Wonder Woman without her even realizing it because he's faster than a speeding bullet. So he swoops down and fucks her, and he's gone in the blink of an eye! Wonder Woman gets up and says, "What the hell was that?" And The Flash says, "I don't know but my ass is killing me."

A man had been dating his girlfriend for over a year when he popped the question. One day, his future sister-in-law called him to come over to her house to check out the wedding invitations.

She was in her mid-twenties, single, and would always wear tight miniskirts and bra-less tops. When the man arrived, his future sister-in-law was alone, and she whispered to him that she had feelings and desires for him that she couldn't overcome. She told him that she wanted him just once before he got married and committed his life to her sister. The man was in total shock, and couldn't say a word. She said, "I'm going upstairs to my bedroom, and if you want one last wild fling, just come up and get me." He was stunned and frozen in shock as he watched her go up the stairs. He stood there for a moment, then turned and made a beeline straight to the front door. He opened the door, and headed straight for his car. All of a sudden, his entire future family was standing outside, all clapping! With tears in his eyes, his new father-in-law hugged him and said, "We are very happy that you have passed our little test. We couldn't ask for a better man for our daughter. Welcome to the family." The moral of this story is: Always keep your condoms in your car.

A mom is driving a little girl to her friend's house for a play date. "Mommy," the little girl asks, "How old are you?" The mother looks over at the little girl, "Honey, you are not supposed to ask a lady her age, it isn't polite." the mother warns. "Okay," the little girl says, "How much do you weigh?" "Now really," the mother says, "These are personal questions and are really none of your business." Undaunted, the little girl asks, "Why did you and daddy get a divorce?" "That is enough questions, honestly!" The exasperated mother walks away as the two friends begin to play. "My mom wouldn't tell me anything," the little girl says to her friend. "Well," said the friend, "All you need to do is look at her driver's license. It is like a report card- it has everything on it." Later that night, after reading her mother's driver's license, the little girl says to her mother, "I know how old you are, you are 32." The mother is surprised and asks, "How did you find that out?" "I also know that you weigh 140 pounds." The mother is shocked now. "How in heavens name did you find that out?" The little girl continues on triumphantly, "And... I know why you and daddy got divorced." "Oh really? The mother asks, "Why is that?" The girl replies, "Because you got an F in sex."

Three mice are sitting in a bar in a pretty rough neighborhood late at night trying to impress each other about how tough they are. The first mouse slams a shot of scotch, and pounds the shot glass to the bar. He to the second mouse and says: "When I see a mousetrap, I get on it, lie on my back, and set it off with my foot. When the bar comes down, I catch it in my teeth, and then bench press it 100 times." The second mouse orders up two shots of tequila. He grabs one in each paw, slams the shots, and pounds the glasses to the bar. He turns to the other mice and replies: "Yeah, well when I see rat poison, I collect as much as I can and take it home. In the morning, I grind it up into a powder and put it in my coffee so I get a good buzz going for the rest of the day." The first mouse and the second mouse then turn to the third mouse. The third mouse lets out a long sigh and says to the first two, "I don't have time for this bullshit. I gotta go home and fuck the cat."

A woman walks into her accountant's office and tells him that she needs to file her taxes. The accountant says, "Before we begin, I'll need to ask a few questions." He gets her name, address, and social security number, and then asks, "What is your occupation?" The woman replies, "I'm a high-priced whore." The accountant balks and says, "No, no, no. That will never work. That is much too crass. Let's try to rephrase that." The woman says, "OK, I'm a high-end call girl!" "No, that is still too crude. Try again." They both think for a minute, then the woman states, "I'm an elite chicken farmer." The accountant asks, "What does chicken farming have to do with being a whore or a call girl?" She replies, "Well, I raised over 5,000 little peckers last year."

A teacher named Ms. Smith found one of her students making

faces at others on the playground. Ms. Smith stopped to gently reprimand the child. Smiling sweetly, the teacher said, "Bobby, when I was a child, I was told if that I made ugly faces, it would freeze and I would stay like that." Bobby looked up and replied, "Well, Ms. Smith, you can't say you weren't warned."

A father and son went to see a doctor since the father was getting very ill. The doctor told the father and son that the father was dying from cancer. The father, who was an Irishman, turned to his son and said, "Son, even on this dark and gloomy day, it is our tradition to drink to health as it is in death, so let's go to the bar and celebrate my demise." Reluctantly, his son follows him to the local bar. There, while enjoying their beers, the father sees some old friends and tells them he is dying from AIDS. Shocked, the son turns to his father and says, "Father, you're not dying from AIDS, you're dying from cancer. Why did you lie to those men?" The father replies, "Aye, you are right, my son; but I don't want those guys sleeping with your mom when I'm gone."

After 40 years as a gynecologist, Matt decided he had enough money to retire and take up his real love- auto mechanics. He left his practice, enrolled in auto mechanics school, and studied hard. The day of the final exam came and Matt worried if he would be able to complete the test with the same proficiency as his younger classmates. Most of the students completed their exam in two hours. Matt, on the other hand, took the entire four hours allotted. The following day, Matt was delighted and surprised to see a score of 150% for his exam. Matt spoke to his professor after class. "I never dreamed I could do this well on the exam. How did I earn a score of 150%?" The professor replied, "I gave you 50% for perfectly disassembling the car engine. I awarded another 50% for perfectly reassembling the engine. I gave you an additional 50% for having done all of it through the muffler."

A woman was shaking out a rug on the balcony of her 17th floor condominium when a sudden gust of wind blew her over the railing. "Damn, that was stupid," she thought as she fell. "What a way to die." As she passed the 14th floor, a man standing at his railing caught her in his arms. While she looked at him in disbelieving gratitude, he asked, "Do you suck?" "No!" she shrieked, aghast. So, he dropped her. As she passed the 12th floor, another man reached out and caught her. "Do you screw?" he asked. "Of course not!" she exclaimed before she could stop herself. He dropped her, too. The poor woman prayed to God for one more chance. As luck would have it, she was caught a third time, by a man on the eighth floor. "I suck! I screw!" she screamed in panic. "Slut!" he screamed, and dropped her.

Two young boys walked into a pharmacy one day, picked out a box of tampons and proceeded to the checkout counter. The man at the counter asked the older boy, "Son, how old are you?" "Eight," the boy replied. The man continued, "do you know what these are used for?" The boy replied, "not exactly, but they aren't for me. They're for him. He's my brother. He's four. We saw on TV that if you use these you would be able to swim and ride a bike. Right now, he can't do either."

A flat-chested young lady went to Dr. Smith for advice about breast enlargements. He told her, "Every day when you get out of the shower, rub the top of your nipples and say, 'Scooby dooby dooby, I want bigger boobies.'" She did this, every day, faithfully. After several months, it worked! She grew great boobs! One morning she was running late, and in her rush to leave for work, she realized she had forgotten her morning ritual. At this point she loved her boobs and didn't want to lose them, so she got up in the middle of the bus and said, "Scooby dooby dooby, I want bigger boobies." A guy sitting nearby asked her, "Do you go to Dr. Smith by any chance?" "Why yes, I do. How did you know?" The man stood up and cupped his crotch and said, "Hickory dickory dock..."

A young, attractive woman thought she might have some fun with a stiff-looking military man at a cocktail party, so she walked over and asked him, "Major, when was the last time you had sex?" "1956," was his reply. "No wonder you look so uptight!" she exclaimed. "Major, you need to get out more!" "I'm not sure I understand you," he answered, glancing at his watch. "It's only 2014 now."

A woman sought the advice of a sex therapist, confiding that she found it increasingly difficult to find a man who could satisfy her, and that it was very wearisome getting in and out of all these short term relationships. "Isn't there some way to judge the size of a man's equipment from the outside?" she asked earnestly. "The only foolproof way, is by the size of his feet," counselled the therapist. So the woman went downtown and proceeded to cruise the streets, until she came across a young fellow standing in an unemployment line with the biggest feet she had ever laid her eyes on. She took him out to dinner, wined and dined him, and then took him back to her apartment for an evening of abandon. When the man woke up the next morning, the woman had already gone but, by the bedside table was a $20 bill and a note that read, "With my compliments, take this money and go out and buy a pair of shoes that fit you."

Tony and his friend John die in a car accident and go to judgment. God tells Tony that because he cheated on his income taxes, the only way he can enter Heaven is to sleep with a stupid, ugly woman for the next five years. A few days later, as Tony's walking in the park with his hideous new girlfriend, he spots his friend John with an absolutely drop dead gorgeous woman. "John, what happened?" Tony asks. "I have no idea," John replies. "I was told I have five years of amazing sex to look forward to. The only thing I don't understand is why she always yells 'Damn income taxes!' whenever we have sex."

A few days after Christmas, a mother was working in the kitchen listening to her young son playing with his new electric train in the living room. She heard the train stop and her son said, "All of you sons of bitches who want off, get the fuck off now, 'cause this is the last stop! And all of you sons of bitches who are getting on, get your asses in the train." The mother went nuts and told her son, "We don't use that kind of language in this house. Now I want you to go to your room and you are to stay there for two hours and think about what you've done." Two hours later, the son comes out of the bedroom and resumes playing with his train. Soon the train stopped and the mother heard her son say, "All passengers who are disembarking from the train, please remember to take all of your belongings with you. We thank you for riding with us today." She hears the little boy continue, "For those of you just boarding, we ask you to stow all of your hand luggage under your seat." As the mother began to smile, the child added, "For those of you pissed about the two-hour delay, please see the cunt in the kitchen!"

A poor man meets a rich man around Christmas. The poor man asks the rich man, "What are you getting your wife this Christmas?" The rich man replies, "Diamond earrings and a Mercedes." The poor man asks, "Why are you getting her two gifts?" The rich man says, "Well, if she doesn't like the earrings she can drive to the store and exchange them." The poor man nods. Then the rich man asks him, "So, what are you getting your wife this year?" The poor man thinks about it for a second and replies, "A pair of slippers and a dildo." The rich man asks, "Why those two things?" The poor man responds, "This way, if she doesn't like the slippers she can go fuck herself."

Two five-year-old boys are standing at the toilet to pee. One says, "Your thing doesn't have any skin on it! "I've been circumcised," the other replied. "What's that mean?" "It means they cut the skin off the end." "How old were you when it was cut off?" "My mom said I was two days old." "Did it hurt?" the kid asked. "You bet it hurt. I didn't walk for a year!"

The judge says to a double-homicide defendant, "You're charged with beating your wife to death with a hammer." A voice at the back of the courtroom yells out, "You bastard." The judge says, "You're also charged with beating your mother-in-law to death with a hammer." The voice in the back of the courtroom yells out, "You God-damned bastard." The judge stops, and says to the guy in the back of the courtroom, "Sir, I can understand your anger and frustration at this crime. But no more outbursts from you, or I'll charge you with contempt. Is that a problem?" The guy in the back of the court stands up and says, "For fifteen years, I've lived next door to that bastard, and every time I asked to borrow a hammer, he said he didn't have one."

This guy walks into the bar and sees a gorgeous blonde sitting on a bar stool all alone. So the guy sits down next to her and pulls a small box from his pocket. He opens it and there's a frog inside. The blonde says, "He's cute, but does he do tricks?" The guy says, "Yea, he licks pussy." After talking with her for several minutes, he convinces her to come with him to his apartment. They get there and she takes all of her clothes off, gets into the bed and spreads her legs. The guy sets the frog right between her legs and it just sits there not moving at all. The blonde says, "Well?" The frog still does not move. So the guy leans over to the frog, and says, "All right, I'm only going to show you how to do this one more time!"

A truck driver is sitting in a restaurant enjoying a pancake breakfast when a gang of bikers come in. After a while they begin to taunt the trucker for his "unmanly" choice of breakfast fare. When they can't get a rise out of him, one big biker walks over and spits in his coffee. Another biker comes over and puts his cigarette out on the trucker's pancakes. And the third biker dumps the coffee onto the trucker's plate. The trucker says nothing, thanks the waitress, pays his bill and leaves. The bikers sit back down and one says, "That guy sure wasn't much of a man." The waitress walks over to their table and says, "Not much of a driver either, he just backed over a bunch of Harley's."

A teacher was wrapping up class, and started talking about tomorrow's final exam. He said there would be no excuses for not showing up tomorrow, barring a dire medical condition or an immediate family member's death. One smartass male student said, "What about extreme sexual exhaustion?" The teacher replied, "Not an excuse- you can use your other hand to write."

A woman and her little boy were walking through a park in New

York and they pass two squirrels having sex. The little boy asks his mom, "Mommy, mommy, what are they doing?" The lady responded, "They're making a sandwich." Then they pass two dogs having sex and the little boy again asks what they were doing. His mother again replied they were making a sandwich. A couple of days later the little boy walks in on his mother and father and said, "Mommy, Daddy, you must be making a sandwich, because Mommy has mayonnaise all over her mouth!"

A salesman in a strange city was feeling horny and wanted release. He inquired for the address of a good house of ill repute. He was told to go to 225 West 42nd St. By mistake, he went to 255 West 42nd St, the office of a podiatrist. Being met by a beautiful woman in a white uniform surprised but intrigued him. She directed him to an examining room and told him to uncover and someone would be with him soon. He loved the thought of the table and the reclining chair, and was really getting aroused because of the strange and different approach this house offered. Finally, the doctor's assistant, a really gorgeous redhead, entered and found him sitting in the chair with his generous member in his hand. "My goodness!" she exclaimed, "I was expecting to see a foot." "Well," he said, "if you're going to complain about an inch then I'll take my business elsewhere."

A depressed young woman was so desperate that she decided to end her life by throwing herself into the ocean. When she went down to the docks, a handsome young sailor noticed her tears, took pity on her, and said, "Look, you've got a lot to live for. I'm off to Europe in the morning, and if you like, I can stow you away on my ship. I'll take good care of you and bring you food every day." Moving closer, he slipped his arm around her shoulder and added, "I'll keep you happy, and you'll keep me happy." The girl nodded yes, after all, what did she have to lose? That night, the sailor brought her aboard and hid her in a lifeboat. From then on, every night he brought her three sandwiches and a piece of fruit, and they made passionate love until dawn. Three weeks later, during a routine search, she was discovered in the lifeboat by the captain. "What are you doing here?" the captain asked. She got up off the ground and explained, "I have an arrangement with one of the sailors. He's taking me to Europe, and he's screwing me." The captain looked at her, "He sure is lady, this is the Staten Island Ferry."

One day when the teacher walked into the classroom, she noticed that someone had written the word "PENIS" in tiny letters on the blackboard. She scanned the class looking for a guilty face. Finding none, she rubbed the word off and began class. The next day, the word "PENIS" was written on the board again; this time it was written about halfway across the board. Again she looked around in vain for the culprit, but could not identify the person, so she erased the board and proceeded with the day's lesson. Every morning for about a week, she went into the classroom and found the same disgusting word written on the board, each day's being larger than the previous one, and each being rubbed off vigorously. At the end of the second week, she walked in expecting to be greeted by the same word on the board but instead found the words: "The more you rub it, the bigger it gets."

A man took his senior father to the mall one day to buy new shoes. They decided to stop in the food court and get lunch. They sat down at a table, and then a group of teenagers sat at the table next to them. The man noticed his father was starting at a teenager who had spiked hair dyed in many colors- green, red, and blue. The man just kept staring at the teenager, who would look up and see the man staring at her. Finally, the teenager had enough, and she sarcastically asked, "What's the matter old man, never done anything wild in your life?" The old man replied without batting an eye: "I got stoned once and screwed a peacock. I was just wondering if you were my daughter."

Three nuns are having tea one morning when the first one says, "I was cleaning the Father's den and found a dirty girl magazine." The second one says, "What did you do?" The first one says, "I tore that filth into small bits and burned it." Then the second one then says, "When I was cleaning the Father's bathroom I found a roll of condoms." "Oh my!" shouts the first one, "What did you do?" The second one says. "I took a needle and poked holes into each one." The third nun fainted.

A dog, a cat, and a penis are sitting around a camp fire one night. The dog says, "My life sucks, my master makes me do my business on a fire hydrant!" The cat says, "My life sucks more. My master makes me do my business in a box of cat litter." The penis outraged, says, "At least your master doesn't put a bag over your head and make you do pushups until you throw up!"

A man goes into a Barnes & Noble Bookstore and asks a young clerk, "Do you have the new book out for men with short penises? I can't remember the title." The clerk replies, "I'm not sure if it's in yet." The man said, "That's the one. I'll take a copy."

Bill Clinton dies and goes straight to hell. When he gets there, the Devil greets him and offers him three ways to spend eternity. They go to the first door and the Devil shows him Newt Gingrich, hanging from the ceiling with fire under him. Bill says "Oh no!

That's not how I want to spend all eternity." They go to the second door. The Devil shows him Rush Limbaugh chained to the wall being tortured. Bill says, "Oh no! Not for me!" They go to the third door. Behind it is Ken Starr, chained to the wall with Monica Lewinsky on her knees giving him a blowjob. Bill thinks and decides, "Hmmm, looks okay to me. I'll take it." The Devil then says, "Good. Hey Monica, you've been replaced."

A dwarf gets on an elevator and pushes the button to go up. Just before the door closes, a hand comes through and opens the door. In steps a very large black man. The dwarf stares and says, "You're the biggest man I have ever seen!" The man nods his head, and replies, "I'm seven feet tall, weigh 259 pounds, and I have 16 inches, I'm Turner Brown." The dwarf faints! After coming too, the dwarf asks the man to repeat himself. So he does, "I said I'm seven foot, 259 pounds, with 16 inches, my name is Turner Brown." The dwarf looks relieved and started laughing. "For a minute there, I thought you said 'Turn Around!"

What is Rodeo Sex? It's when you mount your woman from behind, start going nice and slowly, take her hair, pull her head back slightly, and whisper in her ear: "Your sister was better than you..." and try to hold on for eight seconds!

One day a girl decided to buy some crotch less panties to surprise her boyfriend. She went and bought them, got home, put them on and waited. When the boyfriend got home, there she was, spread eagle on the bed with only her panties and bra on. "Come over here baby," she says smiling. The boyfriend backs off, "If your pussy can do that to your panties - I ain't going anywhere near it!"

An American businessman was in Japan. He hired a local hooker and was going at it all night with her. She kept screaming "Fujifoo, Fugifoo!" which the guy took to be pleasurable. The next day, he was golfing with his Japanese counterparts and he got a hole-in-one. Wanting to impress the clients, he said "Fujifoo." The Japanese clients looked confused and said, "No, you got the right hole."

A man walks down the street and enters a clock and watch shop. While looking around, he notices a gorgeous female clerk behind the counter. He walks up to the counter where she is standing, unzips his pants, flops his penis out and places it on the counter. "What are you doing!" she screams. "This is a clock shop!" He replied, "I know it is, and I would like two hands and a face put on this!"

An army camp in India just received a new commander. During the new commander's first inspection, everything checked out except one thing. There was a camel tied to a tree on the edge of the camp. The commander asked what it was for. One of the soldiers who had been stationed there for a while explained to him that the men sometimes get lonely since there was no woman there, so they have the camel. The commander just let that go, but after a few weeks he was feeling very lonely, so he ordered the men to bring the camel into his tent. The men did, and he went to work on it. After about an hour, the commander came out zipped up his pants and said, "So is that how the other men do it?" One of the men responded, "No, we usually just use the camel to ride into town."

An exhibitionist was taking a trip a train. A female conductor was walking down the aisle collecting tickets. When she got to him, the man opened his coat and exposed himself. The conductor said, "I'm sorry sir. You have to show your ticket here, not your stub."

Tarzan had been living alone in his jungle kingdom for 30 years with only apes for company. To satisfy his needs, he carved shaped holes in trees for sex. Jane, a reporter, came to Africa in search of this legendary figure. Deep in the wilds she came to a clearing and discovered Tarzan vigorously thrusting into a jungle oak. She watched in awe for a while. Finally, overcome by this display of animal passion, Jane came out into the open and offered herself to him. As she reclined on the wild grass, Tarzan ran up to her and gave her a big kick in the crotch. In pain she screamed, "What the hell did you do that for?" Tarzan replied, "Always check for squirrels."

A trumpeter is hired to play two solos in a movie. After the sessions, he is paid handsomely and promised by the director that he will be notified when the movie is released to the public. Three months later, he receives a notice that the movie will make its debut in Times Square at a porno house. The musician enters the theater wearing a dark raincoat and sunglasses so he won't be recognized. Unaccustomed to porno flicks, he sits in the last row next to an elderly couple.   The film has explicit sex scenes: oral intercourse, anal intercourse, and at the end the lead female has sex with ten men.  The musician, who is immensely embarrassed, turns to the elderly couple and whispers, "I wrote the score and I just came to hear the music."  The elderly woman whispers in reply, "We just came to see our daughter star in a movie."

A man was walking through a crowded street fair when he decided to stop and sit at a palm reader's table. The mysterious old woman said, "For fifteen dollars, I can read your love line and tell your romantic future." The man readily agreed and the reader took one look at his open palm and said, "I can see that you have no girlfriend." "That's true," said the man. "Oh my goodness, you are extremely lonely, aren't you?" she said. "Yes," the man shamefully admitted. "That's amazing. Can you tell all of this from my love line?" The palm reader replied, "Love line? No, from the calluses and blisters."

An artist was doing a painting of a naked model. The artist tried to concentrate on his work, but the attraction he felt for his model finally became irresistible. He threw down his palette, took her in his arms, and kissed her. She pushed him away. "Maybe your other models let you kiss them," she said, "but I'm not that kind!" "Actually, I've never tried to kiss a model before," he protested. "Really?" she said, softening. "Well, how many models have there been?" "Four so far," he replied, thinking back. "A jug, two apples and a vase."

A young doctor moved into town and set up a new practice. He had a new sign painted and hung it in front of his office, proclaiming his specialties: "Homosexuals & Hemorrhoids." The town council members were upset with the sign and asked him please to change it. The doctor was eager to please, so he put up a new sign: "Queers & Rears." The town council members were really fuming about that one, so they demanded that the doctor come up with a decent sign that would not offend the townspeople. So the doctor came up with an acceptable sign: "Odds & Ends."

The Madam opened the brothel door to see a frail, elderly gentleman. "Can I help you?" the madam asked. "I want Natalie," the old man replied. "Sir, Natalie is one of our most expensive ladies, perhaps someone else..." "No, I must see Natalie." Just then Natalie appeared and announced to the old man that she charges $1,000 per visit. Without blinking, the man reached into his pocket and handed her ten $100 bills. The two went up to a room for an hour, and then the man calmly left.  The next night he appeared again demanding to see Natalie.  Natalie explained that no one had ever come back two nights in a row and that there were no discounts... it was still $1,000 a visit. Again the old man took out the money, the two went up to the room and an hour later, he left.  When he showed up the third consecutive night, no one could believe it. Again he handed Natalie the money and up to the room they went. At the end of the hour Natalie questioned the old man: "No one has ever used my services three nights in a row. Where are you from?" The old man replied, "I'm from Philadelphia."  "Really?" replied Natalie. "I have family who lives there."  "Yes, I know," said the old man. "Your father died, and I'm your sister's attorney. She asked me to give this $3,000 to you."

Mickey Mouse is sitting at a bar crying his eyes out.  "Don't take it so hard," says the bartender. "So your wife is acting a little silly. So what? It's no big deal." Mickey looks up angrily.  "I didn't say she was acting silly, I said she was FUCKING GOOFY!"

A mother and her son were flying on a plane from Los Angeles to Chicago.  The son, who had been looking out the window, turned to his mother and said, "If big dogs have baby dogs and big cats have baby cats, why don't big planes have baby planes?" The mother, who couldn't think of an answer, told her son to ask the flight attendant.  So, the little boy asked the flight attendant, "If big dogs have baby dogs and big cats have baby cats, why don't big planes have baby planes?" The flight attendant asked, "Did your mother tell you to ask me that?" He said that she had.  With a clever grin, she said, "Tell your mother it's because our airline always pulls out on time."

After a two-year study, the National Science Foundation announced the following results on America's ball-related recreational preferences.  The sport of choice for unemployed or incarcerated people is basketball. The sport of choice for maintenance level employees is bowling. The sport of choice for blue-collar workers is football. The sport of choice for supervisors is baseball. The sport of choice for middle management is tennis. The sport of choice for corporate officers is golf. Conclusion: The higher you rise in the corporate structure, the smaller your balls become.

A redhead walks into a porno shop. She asks, "How much for the white dildo?" The clerk answers, "35 bucks." The redhead asks, "How much for the black one?" The clerk answers, "Same price. $35 for the black one, $35 for the white one." The redhead says, "I think I'll take the black one. I've never had a black one before." She pays him, and off she goes. A little bit later a black woman comes in and asks, "How much for the black dildo?" The clerk says, "35 bucks." The black woman asks, "How much for the white one?" The clerk says, "Same price. $35 for the white one, $35 for the black one." The black woman says, "I'll take the white one. I've never had a white one before." She pays him, and off she goes. About an hour later, a young blonde woman comes in and asks, "How much are your dildos?" The clerk responds, "$35 for the white, $35 for the black." The blonde looks at the shelf and says, "How much is that plaid one?" The clerk responds, "Well, that's a very special dildo. It'll cost you $165." The blonde thinks for a moment and answers, "I'll take the plaid one, I've never had a plaid one before." She pays him, and off she goes. The clerk's boss arrives for the day and asks, "How are sales going?" The clerk responded. " So far so good. I sold one white dildo, one black dildo, and I sold your thermos for $165!"

An elderly man buys an ice cream from an ice cream van for his grandson. The little boy asks, "Crushed nuts granddad?" The man responds, "No, I always walk like this."

A wife comes home early to find her husband fucking a midget in the bathtub. "You promised me you wouldn't cheat on me again!" she screamed. "Calm down!" he replied. "Can't you see I'm trying to cut down?"

A lizard is walking in the forest, and he sees a koala bear up in a tree smoking something. He says, "Hey koala, what are you doing up there?" The koala replies, "Just smoking some pot. Do you want some?" The lizard says, "Sure, why not?" and the lizard proceeds to get high. A while later, the lizard gets thirsty, so he asks the koala what he should do. The koala tells him to go down to the river to get a drink. The lizard does so, and while he's trying to get down there, he falls in and starts drowning. An alligator swims up and saves his life. The alligator asks, "Hey man what are you doing in there? Are you okay?" The lizard replies, "I was just so high from some great weed that I fell in and couldn't figure out where to go. The alligator asks, "Where can I get some of this weed?" And the lizard tells him to talk to the koala. So the alligator goes to the koala. The koala sees the alligator and screams, "Holy shit! How much water did you drink?"

A Texan sitting at a restaurant table notices a gorgeous woman sitting at another table, alone. He calls the waiter over and asks for the most expensive bottle of champagne to be sent over to her knowing that if she accepts it, she is his. The waiter gets the bottle and quickly sends it over to the woman, saying this is from the gentleman. She looks at the champagne and decides to send a note with the bottle back over to the Texan. The note read: "For me to accept this bottle, you need to have a Mercedes in your garage, a million dollars in the bank, and seven inches in your pants." The Texan, after reading this note, sends a note back to her. It read: "Just so you know, I happen to have TWO Mercedes in my garage, and I have over two million dollars in the bank. And I won't cut off two inches, not even for you! Sorry, honey."

A straight guy walks into a bar. He quickly he realizes it's a gay bar. "But what the heck," he says, "I really want a drink." When the gay waiter approaches, he says to the customer, "What's the name of your penis?" The customer says, "Look, I'm not into any of that. I'm straight. All I want is a drink." The gay waiter says, "I'm sorry, but I can't serve you until you tell me the name of your penis. Mine for instance is called 'Nike,' for the slogan, 'Just Do It.' That guy down at the end of the bar calls his 'Snickers,' because 'It really satisfies." The customer looks dumbfounded so the bartender tells him he will give him a second to think it over. The customer asks the man sitting to his left, who is sipping on a beer, "Hey bud, what's the name of your penis?" The man looks back and says with a smile, "Timex." The thirsty customer asks, "Why Timex?" The fella proudly replies, "Cause' it takes a lickin' and keeps on tickin!" A little shaken, the customer turns to the fella on his right, who is sipping a fruity margarita and says, "So, what do you call your penis?" The man turns to him and proudly exclaims, "Ford, because 'Quality is Job 1.' " Then he adds, "Have you driven a Ford, lately?" Even more shaken, the customer has to think for a moment before he comes up with a name for his penis. Finally, he turns to the bartender and exclaims, "The name of my penis is 'Secret.' Now give me my beer." The bartender begins to pour the customer a beer, but with a puzzled look asks, "Why Secret?" The customer says, "Because it's 'Strong enough for a man, but made for a woman!"

Two aliens landed in the Arizona desert near a gas station that was closed for the night. They approached one of the gas pumps and the younger alien addressed it saying, "Greetings, Earthling. We come in peace. Take us to your leader." The gas pump, of course, didn't respond. The younger alien became angry at the lack of response. The older alien said, "I'd calm down if I were you." The younger alien ignored the warning and repeated his greeting. Again, there was no response. Ticked off at the pump's haughty attitude, he drew his ray gun and said gruffly, "Greetings, Earthling. We come in peace. Take us to your leader or I will fire!" The older alien again warned his comrade saying, "You probably don't want to do that! I really think that will make him mad." "Rubbish," replied the cocky, young alien. He aimed his weapon and opened fire. There was a huge explosion. A massive fireball roared towards him and blew the younger alien off his feet and threw him in a burnt, smoking mess about 200 yards away in a cactus patch. When the younger alien regained consciousness, he refocused his three eyes, straightened his bent antenna, and looked dazedly at the older, wiser alien who was standing over him shaking his big, green head. "What a ferocious creature!" exclaimed the young alien. "He almost killed me! How did you know he was so dangerous?" The older alien replied, "If there's one thing I've learned during my intergalactic travels, you never mess with a guy who can loop his pecker over his shoulder twice and then stick it in his ear."

Two little old ladies rode the train every Saturday from Providence, RI to Boston, MA. They would nod to one another but rode in separate cars and never spoke. One day, when the train was crowded, they both happened to sit together. One says to the other, "I've seen you ride this train every Saturday afternoon to Boston and I've always wondered about it. What do you do in Boston?" The other replied, "Why, I go into Boston to get scrod because I can't get it in Providence." The first lady said, "You know, I've been a schoolteacher for 30 years and I never knew what the past tense of that verb was."

Bud and Jim were a couple of drinking buddies who worked as airplane mechanics in Orlando. One day the airport was fogged in and they were stuck in the hangar with nothing to do. Bud said, "Man, I wish we had something to drink!" Jim says, "Me too. I've heard you can drink jet fuel and get a buzz. You want to try it?" They pour themselves a couple of glasses of high octane fuel and get completely smashed. The next morning Bud wakes up and is surprised at how great he feels- no hangover, no side effects at all! Then the phone rings. It's Jim. Jim says, "Hey, how do you feel this morning?" Bud says, "I feel great. How about you?" Jim says, "I feel great, too. You don't have a hangover?" Bud says, "No, that jet fuel is great stuff - no hangover, nothing. We ought to do this more often." Jim says, "Yeah, well there's just one thing..." Bud replies, "What's that?" Jim says, "Have you farted yet?" Bud responds, "No." Jim exclaims, "Well, DON'T, 'cause I'm in PHOENIX!"

Charlie's wife, Lucy, had been after him for several weeks to paint the seat on their toilet. Finally, he got around to doing it while Lucy was out. After finishing, he left to take care of another matter before she returned. She came in and undressed to take a shower. Before getting in the shower, she sat on the toilet. As she tried to stand up, she realized that the not-quite-dry epoxy paint had glued her to the toilet seat. Charlie got home and realized her predicament. They both pushed and pulled without any success whatsoever. Finally, in desperation, Charlie undid the toilet seat bolts. Lucy wrapped a sheet around herself and Charlie drove her to the hospital emergency room. The ER doctor got her into a position where he could figure out how to free her. Lucy tried to lighten the embarrassment of it all by saying, "Well, Doctor, I'll bet you've never seen anything like this before." The doctor replied, "Actually, I've seen lots of them. I've just never seen one mounted and framed."

Two parents take their son on vacation and go to a nude beach. The father goes for a walk on the beach and the son goes to play in the water. Shortly thereafter, the boy runs to his mother and says, "Mommy, I saw some ladies with boobies a lot bigger than yours!" The mother cleverly replies, "The bigger they are, the dumber they are!" With that, the little boy runs back into the water and continues to play. Several minutes later, though, the little boy runs back to his mother and says, "Mommy, I saw some men with dongs a lot bigger than Daddy's!" "The bigger they are, the dumber they are!" she replies. With that, the little boy runs back into the water and continues to play. Several minutes later, though, the little boy runs back to his mother and says, "Mommy, I just saw Daddy talking to the dumbest lady I ever saw and the more he talked, the dumber he got!"

A man had a pet goose. He loved his goose and took it everywhere with him. One day he went to the movies with the goose, and the ticket seller told him that his goose was not allowed in the theater. He ran around the corner and stuffed the goose in his pants. Then he bought his ticket and went into the theater. He picked a seat next to two elderly ladies. During the movie he could hear his goose panting due to lack of air. He unzipped his pants to let the goose breathe. Soon the lady next to him elbowed her friend and whispered, "Esther, Esther you won't believe what's going on next to me. "Esther glances over and says, "Well, you've seen one you've seen them all. " The lady replied, "Well, maybe, but this one's eating my popcorn!"

The Queen of England was visiting one of Canada's top hospitals. During her tour of the floors she passed a room where a male patient was masturbating. "Oh my God!" said the Queen. "That's disgraceful, what is the meaning of this?" The doctor leading the tour explained; "I am sorry your majesty. This man has a very serious condition where the testicles rapidly fill with semen. If he doesn't do that five times a day, they'll explode, and he would die instantly." "Oh dear, I am sorry," said the Queen. On the next floor they passed a room where a young nurse was giving a patient a blow job. "Oh my God!" said the Queen, "What's happening in there?" The doctor replied, "Same problem. Better health plan."

A woman returns home from her husband's memorial service with the urn that contains his ashes. She enters the home, mixes a martini and carries the urn and the drink to the patio where she then sets the urn down on the patio table. She opens the top of the urn, slowly pours out his ashes on the table and thoughtfully and slowly traces her finger through his ashes. She says to the ashes; "Honey, do you remember that convertible that you always promised to buy me for so many years, but never did? Well, with the money from your insurance I bought one and it's beautiful." She proceeds while continuing to slowly trace her finger through the ashes and says: "Dear, do you remember that diamond necklace you always promised to buy me, but never did? Well, with your insurance money I bought one and it's lovely." She continues on with her tracing and then says; "And my dear husband, do you also remember that European cruise you always promised to take me on, but never did? Well, with your insurance money I booked one and I'm leaving in two weeks!"   She then says, "Oh, and by the way dear, do you remember that blow job I always promised to give you, but never did? Well, a promise is a promise, so get ready because here it comes!"

A 92-year-old man went to the doctor one day. The doctor performed his checkup and after all was said and done, the doctor looked at the man and said, "Sir, at 92 years of age you are in the peak of physical health. You are an absolutely perfect specimen. Tell me sir, how are things in your life right now? How is your relationship with your wife?" The old man replied, "Doctor, not only do I have a great relationship with my wife, but I have developed a great relationship with God. See, God knows that I am losing my eyesight. But he has taken mercy on me, and when I get up to go to the bathroom in the middle of the night, God turns on the bathroom light for me. When my business is done, I leave the bathroom, and God turns the light back off for me." The doctor, astounded, calls the man's wife. "Ma'am, your husband is not only in perfect physical condition, but he also told me of his relationship with God. Now, ma'am, is it really true that God turns the light on for him when he goes to the bathroom and then turns the light off after he leaves the bathroom?" The wife lets out a heavy sigh over the phone and tells the doctor, "Aw dammit, he's pissing the refrigerator again!"

Tom, Dick and Harry are walking through the jungle when they get captured by cannibals. The lead cannibal tells them they have a chance to save their lives, but they must go out into the forest and collect three of the same fruit. Tom comes back first with three pomegranates. The lead cannibal tells him that if he can stick all three fruits up his rear without making any facial expressions, he can go. Tom sticks the first two pomegranates slowly without an expression, but he winces on the third one and is killed and eaten. Dick comes up the hill next with three cherries. The lead cannibal tells him the same thing. Dick gets the first two with no problem, but on the third starts laughing hysterically and is killed and eaten. Up in heaven, Tom rushes over to Dick and says, "What happened? You almost had it!" Dick responds, "I couldn't help it! I saw Harry coming up the hill with an armload of pineapples!"

It's the 1950s, and Bobby goes to pick up his date, Peggy Sue. Peggy Sue's father answers the door and invites him in. He asks Bobby what they're planning to do on the date. Bobby politely responds that they'll probably just go to the malt shop or to a drive-in movie. Peggy Sue's father suggests, "Why don't you kids go out and screw? I hear all of the kids are doing it." Bobby is shocked. "Excuse me, sir?" "Oh yes, Peggy Sue really likes to screw. She'll screw all night if we let her." Peggy Sue comes downstairs and announces that she's ready to go. About 20 minutes later, a thoroughly disheveled Peggy Sue rushes back into the house, slams the door behind her, and screams at her father, "Dad! The Twist! It's called the Twist!"

A family is at the dinner table. The son asks his father, "Dad, how many kinds of breasts are there? The father, surprised, answers, "Well, son, there are three kinds of breasts. In her 20s, a woman's breasts are like melons, round and firm. In her 30s to 40s, they are like pears, still nice but hanging a bit. After 50, they are like onions." The son asks, "Onions?" The father replies, "Yes- you see them and they make you cry."

A kindergarten teacher one day is trying to explain to her class the definition of the word "definitely" to them. To make sure the students have a good understanding of the word, she asks them to use it in a sentence. The first student raised his hand and said, "The sky is definitely blue." The teacher said, "Well, that isn't entirely correct, because sometimes it's gray and cloudy." Another student says, "Grass is definitely green." The teacher again replies, "If grass doesn't get enough water it turns brown, so that isn't really correct either." Another student raises his hand and asks the teacher, "Do farts have lumps?" The teacher looked at him and said "No... But that isn't really a question you want to ask in class discussion." So the student replies, "Then I definitely shit in my pants."

A young guy drops off his girlfriend at her home after being out together on a date. When they reach the front door he leans up against the house with one hand and says to her, "How about a blowjob?" She screams, "What! Are you crazy!" "Don't worry, it will be quick," he ensures his girlfriend. She replies, "No! Someone might see us..." He insists, "It's just a small blowjob, and I know you like it." She screams, "No! I said no!" He pleads, "Baby... don't be like that." Suddenly, the girl's younger sister shows up at the door in her nightgown, with her hair a mess, rubbing her eyes. She looks at them and smirks, "Dad says either you blow him, I blow him, or he'll come downstairs and blow the guy himself... but for God's sake tell your boyfriend to take his hand off the intercom."

An old man is walking down the street one afternoon when he sees a woman with perfect breasts. He says to her, "Hey miss, would you let me bite your breasts for $100? She is shocked. "Are you nuts?" she replies, and keeps walking away. He turns around, runs around the block and gets to the corner before she does. "Would you let me bite your breasts for $1,000?" he asks again. She is disgusted and says, "Listen you; I'm not that kind of woman! Got it?" So the little old man runs around the next block and faces her again, "Would you let me bite your breasts - just once - for $10,000?" She thinks about it for a while and says, "Hmm, $10,000... Okay, just once, but not here. Let's go to that dark alley over there." So they go into the alley, where she takes off her blouse to reveal the most perfect breasts in the world. As soon as he sees them, he grabs them and starts caressing them, fondling them slowly, kissing them, licking them, burying his face in them - but not biting them. The woman finally gets annoyed and asks, "Well? Are you going bite them or not?" "Nah," says the little old man as he walks away. "Costs too much!"

A male whale and a female whale were swimming off the coast of Japan when they noticed a whaling ship. The male whale recognized it as the same ship that had harpooned his father many years earlier. He said to the female whale, "Let's both swim under the ship and blow out of our air holes at the same time, and it should cause the ship to turn over and sink." They tried it and sure enough, the ship turned over and quickly sank. Soon however, the whales realized the sailors had jumped overboard and were swimming, heading to the shore. The male was enraged that they were going to get away and told the female, "Let's swim after them and gobble them up before they reach the shore." At this point, he realized the female was becoming reluctant to follow him. "Look," she said, "I went along with the blow job, but I absolutely refuse to swallow the seamen."

Mickey Mouse called the police because someone had written "Mickey Sucks" in urine in the snow in front of Mickey's house. The responding police officer told Mickey, "I've got some good news and I have some bad news." "What's the good news?" Mickey asked. "The good news is that we were able to identify whose urine it was. It was Goofy's." "How could the bad news be worse than that?" "It was Minnie's handwriting."

An alcoholic, a sex addict, and a pothead all die and go to Hell. Satan is waiting for them and tells all of them, "I am in a good mood today, so I am going to let each one of you pick one thing you love from earth and let you keep it here for 100 years, and then I will return for the goods." Satan first approaches the alcoholic, "What is it that you would like to have?" The alcoholic responds, "I want the finest brew, wine and liquor you can get me." Satan brings him to a room filled with every type of beer on tap, the finest wines, and the most expensive, high-quality liquors. The man yells in excitement, and runs into the room. Satan laughs, shuts the door and locks it. Satan then approaches the sex addict and asks, "What is it that you would like to have?" The sex addict responds, "Women! I want lots of beautiful women, one for each day of the year!" Satan brings him to a room filled with the most beautiful women imaginable, all naked and in the mood. The sex addict runs into the room. Satan laughs, shuts the door and locks it. Satan approaches the pothead and asks, "What is it that you would like to have?" and he responds, "Well, that's easy! I want the best pot you got." Satan brings him to a room filled with the tallest, thickest pot bushes ever, and boxes of rolling paper. The pothead was so awed and humbled by the sight of these beautiful plants, that he slowly walked into the room, he sat down Indian style, took slow deep breathes, closed his eyes and proceeded to meditate on this amazing sight. Satan looks at him

164

curiously, shuts the door and locks it. One hundred years pass. Satan returns to the first room with the alcoholic inside, unlocks the door and opens it. There are broken liquor and wine bottles everywhere. The room smells horrid. The alcoholic comes running out with bloodshot eyes. His clothes are covered in his own vomit. He screams, "Help! I don't want it anymore. Let me out of here!" Satan pushes the man pack inside, laughs, shuts the door and locks it. Satan then returns to the second room with the sex addict inside, unlocks and opens the door. There are thousands of kids running around the room and babies crying. Hundreds of old ladies now limp around with no clothes on, still very horny for the sex addict, who attempts to run out the door as Satan watches. Before the sex addict can escape, Satan laughs, shuts the door and locks it. Satan finally arrives at the third room with the pothead inside, unlocks and opens the door. After a quick look inside, Satan's evil grin turns to a look of confusion. Nothing had changed. The plants were untouched. The rolling papers were never used. Even the pothead was in the same position, sitting down with his legs crossed. Satan walks up behind the pothead, taps him on his shoulder and says, "What's wrong?" A tear rolls down the pothead's cheek as he turns to Satan and simply replies, "Got a light, man?"

Made in the USA
Coppell, TX
29 May 2020

26661651R00095